BASIC BELIEFS

BASIC BELIEFS

*An Introductory Guide
to Christian Theology*

by Donald E. Demaray

LIGHT AND LIFE PRESS
Winona Lake, Indiana

To

my father

C. DORR DEMARAY

faithful minister of the Gospel

Preface

Basic Beliefs is intended to be an introductory guide to Christian theology. Its purpose is to aid in understanding the essentials of the Christian faith. In line with this aim, each chapter has been kept simple and brief.

It is becoming the popular thing for churches and colleges to have classes in subjects related to Christian doctrine. This book is designed as a guide for just such situations. Its usefulness, however, should not be limited to group study. The personal needs and interests of Christian people and those interested in learning more about the Christian faith have been kept in view.

The outline method has been used to facilitate both reading and learning. Additional aids are provided at the end of each chapter by way of (1) Scripture passages to be read, (2) several bibliography suggestions, and (3) some keynote questions to stimulate thought and discussion.

It is hoped that this study will help to clarify many aspects of the Christian faith and increase our knowledge of its basic teachings. It is further hoped that the book's emphasis on doctrine will result in consistent Christian behavior and wholesome witnessing to the power of Jesus Christ to change men's lives. The gospel in a "nutshell" is that Christ the Savior can take a bad man and make him good. It is this message we must make clear and proclaim from the housetops to a needy and sinful generation.

E. Walter Helsel, Professor of Religion in Seattle Pacific College, has read the manuscript copy of this book and offered numerous helpful suggestions. His assistance has been greatly appreciated. Four graduate students at the College, Palmer Gordon Brown, Jim Davis, Peter Hori and Lowell Noble, have given valuable suggestions and criticisms.

DONALD E. DEMARAY

Seattle Pacific College
Seattle, Washington
1958

Contents

1

Does God Really Exist?

There are many reasons for believing that God exists. We cannot examine all of these reasons in a single chapter, but some chief arguments are outlined here.

I. THE ARGUMENT FROM CAUSE AND DESIGN

There is a very old argument for the existence of God which has come to be known as the argument from *design* or the *cosmological* argument. It is one of the most convincing of all the ancient philosophic arguments for belief in God. In a word it is this: Our intricately planned world could not have come into being by chance alone; Something or Someone must have made it.

It would be absurd to look at a beautifully constructed house, to admire its functional design, and then say that the house came into being quite by accident, that it had no architect and that no one built it. Likewise it is ridiculous to look about us and observe our beautiful world, operating after skillfully designed laws, and say it all happened by accident.

Trees with their intricate mechanism for feeding and growth, plants with their capacity to produce buds and in turn the full flower — such things could not "just happen." The human body, too, is amazing: birth, continuing existence through the processes of breathing, circulation, and digestion demonstrate that a Creator made our bodies. Of one part of the human body — the eye — Spinoza, the famous philosopher, said that he could not conceive of anyone making a careful examination of the eye and then failing to believe in God. Spinoza was saying that the eye is such a remarkable instrument that it cannot be the product of mere chance. There must be a Designer and Creator of the eye.

Or take, as another example, the thinking mechanism of man. Thought itself is a complex process and could not exist without a Designer behind it. Along this line, C. S. Lewis has fascinated us by presenting the atheist with a serious dilemma. In his book *The Case for Christianity* Lewis says: "Supposing there were no intelligence behind the universe, no creative mind. In that case nobody designed my brain for the purpose of thinking. It is merely that when the atoms inside my skull happen for physical or chemical reasons to arrange themselves in a certain way, this gives me, as a by-product, the sensation I call thought. But if so, how can I trust my own thinking to be true? It's like upsetting a milk jug and hoping that the way the splash arranges itself will give you a map of London. But if I can't trust my own thinking, of course I can't trust the arguments leading to atheism, and therefore have no reason to be an atheist, or anything else. Unless I believe in God, I can't believe in thought; so I can never use thought to disbelieve in God."[1] Yes, God is the Designer of our very

---

[1] C. S. Lewis, *The Case for Christianity* (New York: The Macmillan Company, 1944), p. 32.

thought processes; or to put it the other way around, the fact that thought exists posits the existence of God.

To summarize: God is speaking to us out of His creation, announcing through its amazing design, His own existence. It is no wonder Francis Bacon said, "I had rather believe all the fables in the Talmud and the Koran, than that this universal frame is without a mind." Even Voltaire was forced to burst the bonds of his own skepticism, for he found himself crying, "If God did not exist, it would be necessary to invent him." The difficulty with skepticism is that it asks us to believe too much; it asks us to doubt the existence of a Creator behind the created, it invites us to doubt the existence of a Designer behind the designed. This is why any doctrine that questions belief in God is extremely difficult for man to accept.

A.   Law versus God

But there are some people who remain unconvinced. These people say that it is Law rather than God that makes the world go around. A rose produces a bud and then the full flower, not because there is a God, but because the laws of plant life dictate that the rose behave in this manner. Now it was Sir Isaac Newton who established that the universe is run by a set of laws. Newton, himself a deeply religious person, saw God as the creator and user of these laws and he had no idea that anyone would substitute Law for God. But that is exactly what happened; growth and propagation of life in its varied forms — plant, animal, human — were sooner or later accredited to natural processes more than to God. People suggested that the bud and the full flower were not the product of divine activity so much as the product of already existing laws. By the nineteenth and twentieth centuries this idea was rather widely accepted.

B.   The Current Trend

Today, because of this widespread attitude toward Law, the cosmological argument is convincing to some, but to others, by reasons of training and background, it is less convincing. The fact that today many are unconvinced by this and other arguments for God has caused numerous theologians to re-think their approach to teaching belief in God. Let us note what theologians are now saying (not that these things are necessarily new, but that they are currently being said).

(1)   Scholars in theology are now underscoring the fact that the Bible nowhere attempts to prove God. The Bible *assumes* God from its very opening words, "In the beginning God . . . ." It does not argue for His existence. The Bible does not even attempt to describe God; to Moses, God said only, "I AM THAT I AM" (Exodus 3:14).

(2)   Further, theologians are asking, Who is man to be "proving" God anyway? This same question was long ago asked of Job by one of his three friends, "Canst thou by searching find out God?" (Job 11:7). Man is finite and his reason is finite; man is really incapable of demonstrating God. It is not that we should give up the arguments for God's existence, but that the cosmological and other arguments are not one hundred per cent proof. These arguments are *suggestive,* but do not give final *proof.* Any philosopher is well aware of this fact, because he knows very well that man's reason is not completely dependable.

(3)   Actually it may not be man's task to prove

God. Who then will prove Him? God Himself will do so! He only is capable of demonstrating Himself. When someone suggests that God does not exist, maybe, say the theologians nowadays, we do not have to be ready with arguments as we once were. What St. Jerome said of Christ — "Let the Lion out of the cage, He will defend Himself" — is true of God too. Arguments against the agnostic or atheist only result in more arguments from them against God. Perhaps man's arguments for God actually get in the way of Deity trying to prove Himself; perhaps *silence* is the best argument man can give in refutation.

(4)   But if we leave the Lion to defend Himself, just how will He go about doing it? We can be satisfied that God is using all the means at His disposal to reveal Himself. God gave us the Bible, He calls preachers to declare His truths, and He sent His Son to reveal Himself to us. The Bible is the *written Word,* preachers give us the *spoken* Word today, and Christ is the *living* Word. In each case the Word is about God, declaring His existence. Who can come under the illuminating influence of the Bible and doubt God? Who can listen — not with the ears only but also with the heart — to sound gospel preaching and go away saying God does not exist? Who can know Christ as a living Person and question that God is?

And beyond these three — the Bible, preaching, Christ — God is declaring Himself; in fact, He is using every human experience to announce and reveal Himself. And we could add, if man does not get the message, it is his own fault, not God's.

(5)   Now all this has brought us to the matter of

personal faith. How do I know there is a God? Because I have *faith* in Him. But someone argues, I cannot believe He exists and I cannot have faith in something that does not exist. Ah! that is just the point. To someone *outside* the Christian fellowship, it is hard if not impossible to believe fully in God. That is why the argument from design is so frequently unconvincing to the non-believer but so satisfying to the Christian. The non-believer's spiritual eyes are covered with scales and he cannot "see" God. But the believer is no longer blinded; faith is now easy; it is natural (I Corinthians 2:9–12).

This brings us face to face with the theological dictum that faith must come before reason. It is not that reason serves no function but that reason cannot function properly until faith gives it proper direction. Reason without faith cannot lead to anything like a full religious understanding. This is why Anselm said, "I believe in order to understand." With him belief or faith made possible the right use of reason and led to understanding.

II. THE MORAL ARGUMENT

Did you ever stop to wonder how you got your idea of right and wrong? Here is another question: Did you know that people all over the world and down through history have had an idea of right and wrong? Well, they did and do, and the ancients identified this fact with what they called Natural Law. They suggested that by "Nature" all men had a sense of right and wrong. To be sure, a minority did not have this sense, but such people were the exception, just as color-blind people or tone-deaf people are the exception. But normal people down through the ages have had a general idea of what is right and what is wrong.

True, right and wrong have been variously defined through the ages and among various civilizations. But everyone has had some idea of right and wrong; that is, the right-and-wrong concept itself has always existed. And it is amazing how similar the codes of ethics have been through the centuries and among cultures. People have always had a pretty good idea that murder, promiscuity and thievery were wrong, and that all that goes into making for fair play was right.

Now where did we get this knowledge of right and wrong? The answer to that question is, God.

A. Moral Knowledge and Instinct

But some have suggested that moral knowledge is not from God at all, that it is one of the instincts. C. S. Lewis says that moral knowledge is not an instinct such as self-preservation but a quality of the personality or soul. When one sees a drowning man, says Lewis, two instincts come immediately into play: the one is to save the man, the other is to protect oneself. But there is a third factor that comes into the picture shortly thereafter; it is the higher call that one *must* help the man who is drowning. This higher call is a sense of *obligation*. This third factor is distinct from the first two factors; it is a moral factor, while the other two are purely instinctive.

A sense of moral obligation is not an instinct. It is a quality of the human spirit, planted in man by God Himself, and is therefore a proof of God. Even if it were an instinct, we would still have to answer the question of where the instinct came from.

17

B. Moral Knowledge and Education

There are still others who say that moral knowledge is not from God so much as from education. We are taught right and wrong in the home, in school and in church; by ancestors, parents, friends, and relatives; through the books we read, etc. This is all very true. But this does not answer the question as to the origin of right and wrong and of the right-and-wrong concept itself. Where did our ancestors get the idea in the first place so that they could pass the teaching on to us?

Kant, the great philosopher, said that there were two things that never ceased to amaze him: the one was the starry heavens above (that suggests the cosmological argument we discussed above); the other was the moral law within. This same amazement moved the inspired poet to pen Psalm 19. Read it! It is this moral law within every man — this sense of "oughtness" — which is no mere product of education, but the gift of God. If it is the gift of God, God must exist to give it.

NOTE TO CHAPTER 1

The four "classical" arguments for God's existence are listed below. The relation of the first two to what has been called in this chapter "The Argument from Cause and Design" will be seen immediately. The third argument is complex, but mentioned here, and the fourth argument has been outlined in this chapter.

1. The COSMOLOGICAL argument has reference to the *cause* of the universe (KOSMOS is Greek for "universe" or "world"). There must be a cause for what is — the universe and world and all they contain — and that cause, we believe, is God.

2. The TELEOLOGICAL argument points up the presence of *purpose* in our world: water is for drinking, sun is for light, fruit is for food, etc. TELOS is Greek for *end* or *purpose*. Everything has a real purpose; this fact posits a

Designer behind these purposeful things in our purposeful world and universe. (See the Psalms, especially Psalm 104.)

3. The ONTOLOGICAL argument is rather difficult, but has always carried weight. Anselm, an eleventh and twelfth century saint, gave probably the best expression to this argument: "The idea of perfection includes existence, for that which does not exist will be less than perfect; therefore, since we have the idea of a perfect being, that being must exist for the idea includes his being or he would be less than perfect."

4. The MORAL argument (explained in this first chapter) briefly stated, is that there must be a God (a Cause) to account for the sense of right and wrong within every man. Man can recognize good, duty, and a moral law only because there is a God Who Himself has put within every man this capacity for moral recognition.

1. Scripture Readings

To be read: Genesis 1 and 2; Exodus 3:13–17; I Corinthians 2:9–12; Psalm 19; Psalm 104.

2. Bibliography

Hutchins, Robert M., Editor. *Great Books of the Western World.* Chicago: Encyclopedia Britannica, Inc., 1952. Vol. 19. *The Summa Theologica of Saint Thomas Aquinas,* Vol. I, pp. 10–14.

Lewis, C. S. *Mere Christianity.* Glasgow: Fontana Books, 1955. The entire book is one of the best introductions to Christian doctrine in the English language and is shot through with evidence for God's existence. See especially Book I.

————. *The Case for Christianity.* New York: The Macmillan Co., 1944. Part I, chapter IV; Part II, chapter I.

Moule, H. C. G. *Outlines of Christian Doctrine.* London: Hodder and Stoughton, 1892. Chapter II.

Whale, J. S. *Christian Doctrine.* New York: The Macmillan Company, 1941. Chapter I.

Wiley, H. Orton. *Christian Theology.* Kansas City, Missouri: The Beacon Hill Press, 1940. Vol. I, chapter IX.

3. Questions for Discussion

1. Why does the existence of thought suggest to us the existence of a God?
2. Do you agree with Spinoza that the existence of the eye points to the existence of God? (Some would say that the eye is the product of centuries of development rather than the direct product of God.)
3. Distinguish between Law and God.
4. How would you answer a person who was eager to argue against the existence of God?
5. Do you really think God is using every means at His disposal to reveal Himself to us?
6. Why is it often difficult for a person who has not been born again to believe that God exists?
7. What is the moral argument and how does it help us believe in the existence of God?

2

Who Is God?

To ask the question, "Who is God?" is to ask a very big question indeed. In fact, it cannot be answered completely. Our knowledge of God is fragmentary, for God Himself is other, *transcendent,* as we say in theology. That is to say, He is "far away" and hard to "pin down" for specific information. To know God is not as simple as to say two and two make four. To know God is always complex, and if we did not have the Bible, and Nature, and especially Jesus Christ Who came to show us what God is like, we would have no information about God at all.

But let us see just what we do know about God.

I. GOD IS ONE, PERFECT, PERSONAL SPIRIT

For one thing, we know that God is one, perfect, personal Spirit. Let us break that sentence down into its component parts and analyze it.

A. God Is Spirit

The Bible nowhere attempts to define God. The closest it comes to a description of God is in the story in John 4 where Jesus speaks to the woman at the well and says, "God is spirit . . . and those who worship Him must worship in spirit and in truth" (vs. 24). Now a spirit is real but invisible; and the Spirit of God is personal. Sometimes we think of a spirit as a kind of vapor because we cannot see it, but God's Spirit is no mere ethereal something; His Spirit is real for He is the source of Reality.

B.   God Is a Personal Spirit

God is a personal, intelligent, moral being. Both nature and Scripture lead us to this conclusion. He is rational, that is, capable of directing His own activities and of thinking for Himself. David saw this very clearly and exclaimed: "He hath done whatsoever he hath pleased" (Ps. 115:3). His activity is consistently described as purposive — i.e., there is a reason for whatever He does — and this proves His intelligence and therefore His personality. Also proving His personality, is the fact that He made men persons: man, made in God's image (Gen. 1:26, 27), is a person: a non-personal God would have been incapable of making persons. Further, He is represented in Scripture as a Person, "walking" and "talking" and communing with His children.

Now it is extremely important that we think of God as personal. He is not, as someone has described Him, a sort of "oblong blur." He is alive, personally concerned with our problems; He hears and answers our prayers; there is nothing that concerns Him more than our individual and very personal needs. He is not some vague, creative, developing, struggling, suffering force in the universe who is non-personal and therefore quite incapable of entering into our sorrows and joys. We can walk and talk with God.

C. God Is a Perfect, Personal Spirit

Now we add the dimension of perfection. God is absolutely holy, entirely righteous, completely good: in a word, He is perfect. There is none like Him. Cried Moses, "Who is like thee, glorious in holiness, fearful in praises, doing wonders?" He was, of course, referring to God (Exodus 15:11). In His perfection, God is to be distinguished from the world of nature and from His creatures, which are all imperfect. But His virtues are numberless, and He has not the slightest imperfection in Him.

D. God Is One, Perfect, Personal Spirit

We come now to the last dimension — God's oneness. God is not many, He is one. There is what we call the doctrine of polytheism. "Poly" means "many," and the people who embrace this doctrine say that there is not one, but there are many gods. Some of the pagan religions of Asia have thousands and even millions of gods. But Christians believe in only one God. They know that the Bible from beginning to end reveals that there is only one God, and repeatedly says so very specifically, as in Isaiah 43:10, "Before me there was no God formed, neither shall there be after me."

There are others who believe in pantheism. "Pan" means "all," and this doctrine says that God is all and all is God. This makes God a sort of vague, impersonal "all," including nature, and man with his mind, and everything else in the world and universe. But the Bible clearly teaches that God is a unit unto Himself and that the world of nature and the mind of man and his men are the creation of God, separate and distinct from the one true God.

God is simple, that is, He is composed not of parts but of a unit. He is not complex ("many-parted"), but one. He "hangs together." He is absolute truth, life, light, love, and all these are characteristics of but one true God. In essence and nature, He is a unity. "Hear, O Israel, The Lord our God is one Lord" (Deut. 6:4).

II. GOD'S NAMES HELP "GIVE HIM AWAY"

Even as a person's names tend to "give him away," that is, tell us something about him — what he is, who he is, and what he is like — so God's names tell us something about Himself. Let us look at these names as they appear in the Hebrew Old Testament and in the Greek New Testament.

A. 'El or 'Elohim

This is a Hebrew name for God, emphasizing His transcendence or His otherness, and His high and exalted nature. He is of the essence of strength and might, the exalted One, and therefore to be feared.

B. 'Elyon

This is another Hebrew name in the Old Testament. This also underscores the exalted character of God and reminds us that He is the sole object of reverence and worship.

C. 'Adonai

This is the name for "Lord" and indicates, naturally, the Lordship of God over His people. He must be the Master — to use everyday language, the Boss — and 'Adonai is the term most frequently used in addressing God.

D. Shaddai or El-Shaddai

This is an intimate name, indicating God's willingness to become friends with His children. It shows His very personal interest in us and His desire to bless and comfort us. It means some other things too but especially has this warm, personal connotation.

E.   Jehovah

Jehovah or Yahweh is, of course, a very common term for God in the Old Testament. This name reveals that God is gracious and that He will, in fact, help His children. This was the most sacred of the names for God and means quite literally the verb "to be," for He is the essence of being, unchangeable, infinite. He is at the same time concerned with His children and wants very much to have happy relationships with us.

F.   Theos

Theos is the ordinary Greek New Testament word for God. This is the God Christ came to make known; this is the God who loves His children and wants to help them. *Theos* could be taken as the equivalent for Elohim, Elyon, or Shaddai.

G.   Kurios

Kurios is the common Greek word for "Lord" and is equivalent to Adonai and Jehovah.

H.   Pater

Pater, as in Latin, means "Father." This term is used of "God as the creator of all beings (cf. Eph. 3:14,15), the fountain and origin of all life, and, among other beings, of our Lord Jesus Christ, who is in a special sense . . . *the Son,* of the Father (cf, especially John). He is sometimes spoken of as the Heavenly Father, the Father in the Heavens (e.g., Matt. 5:16), as distinguished from

25

earthly fathers."[1] Of God the Father as Creator see such passages as I Corinthians 8:6 and Hebrews 12:9.

III. GOD'S CHARACTERISTICS ALSO HELP "GIVE HIM AWAY"

There are some characteristics or attributes we know God possesses. These, too, help reveal Him to us.

A. God Is Self-Contained

For one thing, God is self-contained; that is, He exists with dependence upon no other creature or thing. He is independent and self-existent: "Neither is worshipped with men's hands, as though he needed anything, seeing he giveth to all life, and breath, and all things" (Acts 17:25).

B. God Is Changeless

For another thing, we know that God is changeless (Mal. 3:6). He is always the same, yesterday, today, and forever (Hebrews 13:8). His perfections, purposes, and promises are eternal! There is movement in God but no change. In those passages that speak of God repenting that He had made man, etc., this is apparently a human, not a divine, way of speaking, for the Bible itself tells us that God "is not a man, that he should repent" (I Sam. 15:29).

C. God Is "Perfection Personified"

We sometimes say he or she is "perfection personified." By that we mean that that person is "really something," ideal. But with God this is no mere expression;

---

[1] Alexander Souter, *A Pocket Lexicon to the Greek New Testament* (London: Oxford University Press, 1916), pp. 195-196.

it is fact. God knows all (Acts 15:18); He is absolutely good (Mark 10:18); He is perfectly loving (I John 4:8, 16). There are no limitations or defections in God. He is in fact Perfection Personified.

D. God Is Eternal

God is eternal; He is the Alpha (beginning) and the Omega (ending).[2] Before Him was not anything made that was made (John 1). He transcends time. There is no beginning or ending with Him. This is a concept too difficult for us finite men to grasp. It is difficult because we have had a beginning in birth and will have an earthly ending in death. Moreover, everything we know has had a beginning and has had or will have an ending. But God is without beginning or ending. He is eternal. Said the Psalmist: "The Lord shall endure forever" (Ps. 9:7); "thou art from everlasting" (Ps. 93:2).

E. God Is Omnipresent

"Omni" means "all" or "every." God is everywhere present all at once: "Do not I fill heaven and earth? saith the Lord" (Jer. 23:23). Even as He transcends time, so He transcends space but is in time and in space. He is not half here or half there; He is at once here and there and everywhere. This is why we can say God sees, hears, and knows everything; because He is everywhere at the same time to see, hear, and know everything. This doctrine is called the Immanence of God. It is graphically described in Psalm 139.

---

[2] Alpha and Omega are the first and last letters of the Greek alphabet.

F.   God Is Omniscient

We have again the prefix "omni" ("all" or "every") plus the suffix, "science" (knowledge). Thus God is all-knowing. "The eyes of the Lord are in every place, beholding the evil and the good" (Prov. 15:3). God knows everything past, present, and future. "Known unto God are all his works from the beginning of the world" (Acts 15:18). He is perfect in His knowledge, and He will always have knowledge of everything. In other words, "his understanding is infinite" (Ps. 147:5).

G.   God Is Love

The Bible says "God is Love" (I John 4:8). God is not a mere emotion, but the very essence of love is contained in God. God really loves or cares about us, His children. That is why He is so willing to make His grace operative in us; that is why He is so anxious to be merciful to us, forgiving our sins; that is why He is so ready to be patient with us no matter how often we have done wrong.

H.   God Is Just

If God is loving, He is also just. "A God of truth and without iniquity, just and right is he" (Deut. 32:4). He must be just because He cannot allow wrong to go unpunished. If one breaks a moral law, the offender must be punished in one way or another for breaking that law. If God were not just, He could not be righteous; and if He were not righteous, He could not be loving.

I.   God Is Sovereign

God is the Sovereign of the universe. "Say among the heathen that the Lord reigneth" (Ps. 96:10). No being or thing or creature is as high and mighty, so much a ruler, as God Himself. He is the King of His Kingdom and of the kingdoms of this world. He is the Commanding General, directing the affairs of this world, for He controls history and individuals within the context of man's freedom. But even when man misuses his freedom and does wrong, God, in spite of man, takes that wrong act and weaves it into the fabric of His eternal plan for His world and universe. When Joseph's brothers sold him into Egypt, God used this cruel deed "to keep much people alive" when a famine struck Palestine (cf. Gen. 50:20). When religious persecution made life difficult in Europe, the Pilgrims came to America and founded a new nation.

IV. GOD IS THREE IN ONE

Yes, that is right! God is three in one. This is called the doctrine of the Trinity, and we believe it, not because it makes good or bad sense, but because it is taught in Scripture and in the history of the Church.

A. Some False Explanations

There have been many attempts to explain the Trinity. Some have said that God plays three different roles at different times: at one time He plays the role of the Father, at another time He puts on the mask of the Son, and at still another time He reveals Himself as Spirit. This false doctrine is called Sabellianism.

Others have said that the Trinitarian idea is not true at all, that God is the Heavenly Father, that the Son was a mere man, and that the Spirit is merely the divine influence. Today this false doctrine is called Unitarianism, but a few centuries ago it was called Socinianism. Many modernists or liberals believe this or a variation of this view today.

But if we are to face the facts squarely, we must say that the Trinity cannot be explained; that it is to be accepted as theological fact, and especially it is to be experienced, for we can know the Father's love, the Son's salvation, and the Spirit's guidance.

B. Based in the Holy Scriptures

The doctrine of the Trinity is based in the Bible. God is referred to as a Spirit (e.g., Isaiah 48:16 and 63:10) and also as more than one person (Isaiah 48:16; 63:9, 10). In the New Testament, the Trinity is revealed with greater clarity in such a passage as Matthew 28:19 (the Great Commission) or in the blessing of II Corinthians 13:14 where Father, Son, and Holy Spirit are distinctly related. At the Baptism of Christ (Matthew 3:16–17) and in the teaching of Christ (John 14:16) the Trinity is made clear. The New Testament sets forth a Father as God (Romans 1:7), a Son as God (Hebrews 1:8), a Spirit as God (Acts 5:3–4). And yet the Bible repeatedly tells us that there is only one God. This *tri-unity* we call the Trinity.

1. Scripture Readings

To be read: John 4:16–26; Exodus 15:1–18; Ephesians 3:14–21; John 1:1–18.

2. Bibliography

Berkhof, Louis, *Manual of Christian Doctrine.* Grand Rapids: Eerdmans, 1953. Pp. 53–89.

Burnabey, John, Editor. *Augustine. Later Works,* in "The Library of Christian Classics." Philadelphia: The Westminster Press, 1955.
Introduction (by John Burnabey) especially, and "The Trinity" by Augustine (pp. 37–181).

Moule, H. C. G. *Outlines of Christian Doctrine*. London: Hodder and Stoughton, 1892. Chapters II and III.

Wiley, H. Orton. *Christian Theology*. Kansas City, Missouri: The Beacon Hill Press, 1940. Vol. I, pp. 217–439.

3. Questions for Discussion

1. How would your theology be changed if you believed in a vague, impersonal God?
2. How do the names for God help "give Him away?"
3. Can you remember the characteristics or attributes of God?
4. What is the Trinity? What are some false explanations of it?

God and Christian Doctrine

John S. Whale and other theologians have pointed out that every Christian doctrine presupposes and illustrates the fact that God exists. Let us take some of our major beliefs and observe how each one is based upon God's existence.

I. THE DOCTRINE OF MAN

In theology we call the study of the doctrine of man *anthropology*. This word comes from two Greek words, *anthropos* and *logos*. *Anthropos* means "man," and *logos* means "a word" or a "discourse." Anthropology, as a branch of theology, is *a word about man,* that is, *a discourse or study about man,* his real nature and character and his behavior.

Now this doctrine would not make sense without the doctrine of God. In our study of anthropology we distinguish between man and the other creatures of our world. Man is no mere animal; he is different. He is a special creation; he has, in fact, qualities which are called "the image of God." This is exactly what the Bible tells us (Gen. 1:26, 27). He is a person with a spirit created in some sense after the likeness of God, for He, too, is a Person with a Spirit. In a word, the existence of man presupposes the existence of God.

II. THE DOCTRINE OF SIN

The doctrine of sin is called *hamartiology*. This term comes from the Greek words *hamartia* and, of course, *logos*. *Hamartia* literally means, "missing the mark." You can see in your mind's eye an archer taking up his bow and arrow; he aims for the center of his target; if he misses, we say he has missed the mark. When we sin we know we have missed the mark of the purity of life God intended for us. Sin is doing something wrong when you know you should have done right.

Now the question arises, "How do we know what the mark is at which we should be aiming?" How do we know what "missing the mark" really means? We know this because of the righteousness of God described to us in Scripture. Sin can be recognized as sin because it is seen in contrast to the righteousness of God. It is by the contrast of man's impurity against God's purity that we know anything about sin at all. Besides, God in Scripture reveals His will for man's life. This points up the meaning of missing the mark, and it makes clear that purity of life is the mark for which we are to aim.

In fact, if sin could not be viewed in contrast to God, it could not be recognized at all. Imagine a painting of a man, but with no other objects in the picture. The viewer would have no way of telling whether the man was short or tall, thin or heavy. It is the contrast provided by the surroundings and background that reveals the size and shape of the man. By the same token, it is the background of the righteousness of God which lays bare the sin of man,

III. THE DOCTRINE OF SALVATION

In theology we know the doctrine of salvation by *soteria* and *logos*. *Soteria* means "health" and, when applied in the theological sense, has the idea of recovery to health from the disease of sin. Now when a person is sick bodily, he calls the doctor; he cannot cause his own health to return without medical assistance. Likewise, when man is plagued with the disease of sin, he cannot cure himself. It is clear that there could be no salvation from sin if there were no God to effect the cure and restore spiritual health.

C. E. M. Joad, famed British philosopher, was, for many years, an agnostic; that is, he could not say for certain that he believed in God. Then one day — during the War when the Nazis were torturing the Jews — he suddenly realized that man was so very wicked that he could not save himself from his own wickedness. He might have learned this from the Bible (Rom. 3:10–12 and elsewhere), but up to this time Professor Joad had accepted the usual arguments of psychology and sociology that sin is the product of mental, emotional, and social maladjustment. But when the gigantic cruelty of man dawned on him, he had to change his way of thinking about sin. It no longer made sense to him that a Nazi torturing a Jew, in every instance, or even in most instances, did so because of childhood repressions or frustrating circumstances. No, the roots of such wretched behavior were far deeper; wickedness was, to use Joad's own term, "endemic," that is, *inherent*. He concluded that evil was so engrained in man that man himself could not make himself good. He concluded further that only one Person in the universe could make a bad man good; that Person was, of course, God.

The truth is plain: man is caught up hopelessly in the cycle of sin; he cannot save himself from that cycle; only God can do that. And when we actually see a sinner released from his own hopeless situation and observe the radical change in him, we cannot doubt God's existence!

IV. THE DOCTRINE OF CHRIST

We call the doctrine of Christ *Christology*. It means simply *the study about Christ*.

In a word, what is our Christian view of Jesus Christ? Well, it is this: He was more than a great teacher such as Socrates, Plato, or Aristotle; He was even more than the founder of a religion, such as Buddha, Zoroaster, or Mohammed. He was in fact the divine Son of God. The Scriptures repeatedly speak of Jesus as the Son of God (cf. Mark 1:1; 9:7; John 8:36; and other places). This accounts for the fact that He was the only perfect man who ever lived; indeed, a perfect person could not have existed unless he had been God Incarnate. Certainly no mere man could have been perfect; moreover, no ordinary man ever has been absolutely perfect. You will search in vain for such a perfect man other than Jesus Christ. Now the Incarnation was God become man, a perfect man, and it is perfectly clear that the Incarnation would have been quite impossible without God. Thus, Christ, like the other doctrines, presupposes and is based in the fact of God's existence.

V. THE DOCTRINE OF THE CHURCH

In theology the doctrine of the Church is known as *ecclesiology*. This term comes from the Greek words *ecclesia* and, of course, *logos*. Logos means "a word" or "discourse." *Ecclesia* means literally "a calling out" and has reference to all those who have been called out of the world by the Spirit of God and, by virtue of their salvation from sin and the world, have been made a part of the Church of Jesus Christ. Paul stresses this when he addresses the members of the Church at Rome: "the called of Jesus Christ: To all that be in Rome, beloved of God, called to be saints" (Rom. 1:6, 7).

This word *ecclesia* really suggests the true nature of the Church. The Church is no mere get-together club; it is more than a nice building on the corner, where good people go on Sunday to hear some pleasing words and sing some pretty songs. Far more meaningful than that, the Church is made up of the redeemed ("saints," as they are repeatedly called in the New Testament); and it is the divinely ordained institution for bringing others into the fellowship of the redeemed (as Jesus stated in his parting words, "Ye shall be witnesses unto me . . ."). The Church is sacred — it is no secular institution! — because it was established by God in Christ and sanctified by His Holy Spirit (cf. Acts 20:32; 26:18; Rom. 15:16; Jude 1); and the Church is preserved and continues by the power of His grace ("kept by the power of God," I Peter 1:5; "preserved in Jesus Christ," Jude 1).

If all this is true — and we believe it is — God must exist, for the Church could not have been established nor could it have become what it is without God. The Church *could* not exist if God *does* not exist.

VI. THE DOCTRINE OF LAST THINGS

Eschatology is a word we hear frequently today; even the newspapers and magazines talk about it. Eschatology comes from two Greek words, *eschatos* and *logos*. *Eschatos* has to do with "last" or "end" things; thus eschatology is *the study of last things*. The "last things" we think of in theology are the Second Coming of Christ, the Last Judgment, and all those things we associate with the winding up of history in the last days.

The real core of the Christian view of eschatology is this: God controls history and will come again in the person of His Son to wind up history. Said the angels to the disciples, "This same Jesus . . . shall so come in like manner as ye have seen him go into heaven" (Acts 1:11). God will wind up His purposes in history in His own time and fulfill His purposes in His world. But why do we leave the control of history to God? Why not let man steer the course of history and make something good out of it? Simply because, as Professor Joad discovered and as Scripture teaches, man in himself has no power to do good (Rom. 3:12). Any good that man does is done because God is in him, helping him to do good. "It is God which worketh in you both to will and to do of his good pleasure" (Phil. 2:13). Man, therefore, cannot in himself handle history; in fact, he has tried throughout the centuries and he has failed (usually in an awful war) every time.

Now if history is, in fact, being directed to some worthy end and if man alone is incapable of directing it to that end, then there must be a God. History could not be controlled if there were no God, for only God is capable of directing history.

Summary

In this section we have discussed the relation of all doctrines to the basic doctrine of God's existence. Every

Christian doctrine is based on the belief that God exists. Whether it be the doctrine of man, salvation, Christ, the Church, last things, or any other, it is clear that not a single doctrine could make sense if God did not exist. One Christian scholar has put it this way: All Christian doctrines are the same doctrine, and that doctrine is the doctrine of God.

1. Bibliography

Whale, J. S. *Christian Doctrine.* New York: The Macmillan Company, 1941. Chapter 1.

2. Questions for Discussion

1. Define the doctrines of man, sin, salvation, Christ, the Church, and eschatology.
2. How is each of the above doctrines grounded in the basic doctrine of God's existence?

4

The Bible,
A Divine Communication

Our word "Bible" comes from the original word for book, *biblios,* a word derived from the ancient Syrian city, Byblos, because the people of this city and area knew much about writing and writing materials. Before the idea of a book[1] was conceived, *biblios* meant papyrus. Papyrus was a reed which grew well along the banks of the Nile River — especially there — and was pounded out into paper-like material for writing. (Thus the ancients often called a document a "papyrus.") Later, after the book idea was thought of, *biblios* meant book.

Now our word Bible comes from *biblios* and thus means, quite literally, a "book." But the Bible is no ordinary book. It took hundreds of years to complete it; yet its redemptive theme runs throughout. The Old Testament was written in Hebrew and the New in *Koine* (market-place) Greek. *Koine* means common; thus the

---

[1] The technical term for "book" is *codex.* Thus the ancient book manuscripts of the Bible are called Codex Alexandrinus, Codex Vaticanus, etc.

Greek of the New Testament was the language of the common man. Added to the Hebrew and Greek, there is a sprinkling of Aramaic (a dialect of Hebrew), which, by the way, was the language Jesus spoke. Further, the Bible contains an amazing variety of literary forms: poetry, drama, informal letters, history, etc.

These are just some of the facts that make the Bible an extraordinary book. But the fact that God communicated to man through this Bible is even more the reason for its uncommon character. It is this fact of divine communication through a book that we want to consider in this chapter.

I. THE BIBLE AS DIVINE COMMUNICATION

The Bible is special because it is *revealed truth.* Revealed truth is given by God. When we use the term "revelation," we mean communication — God communicating to man. Now God uses many means of communicating or revealing Himself to us: nature, preaching, Jesus Christ in history and in His Church today; in fact, God uses every experience of man to try to communicate Himself. The Bible is one of the means God uses in the attempt to communicate. It is a very important and special means because it is an authoritative and unique record about God. Someone has called the Bible "God's special delivery letter to man"; that is a rather simple way of putting it but reflects the profound truth that the Bible is God's Word, His communication, to us, His children.

A. The Holy Spirit, Agent in Communication

The dynamic of the Bible is revealed when the Holy Spirit illuminates the sacred pages to the reader.

When this happens — that is, when the dynamic or power of the Bible is *experienced* — the Bible can be no ordinary book; it is truly *extraordinary* and therefore authoritative. The Bible may be an entertaining book or, at best, a volume of ideals: but when the Holy Spirit clarifies it and drives it home, it is alive! The Holy Spirit inflames the Bible and writes its truths on our hearts.

This truth, that the Bible really communicates God's Word to us when the Holy Spirit illuminates its pages, points up a simple but absolutely necessary principle about Bible reading procedure. When we read the Bible either for study or devotional purposes, *it must be approached in prayer and calm readiness of heart.* The true Christian should never read God's Word without first breathing a prayer for understanding which is given by the Holy Spirit, the divine Illuminator. One cannot expect the Bible to yield its rich stores of truth if it is approached "on the run," or out of a sense of hurried duty.

B.   An Inspired Vehicle of Communication

The term "inspired" means literally, "in-breathed." Thus, God breathed Himself or His thoughts into the Bible. Now if God actually did that — and we believe He did by guiding the writers (see, for example, I Corinthians 2:13) — the Bible must be a highly important document. It is so important, in fact, that it will not do simply to have one in the house or even on your desk. Your aim in possessing a Bible is not to impress your friends with your piety but to let the Bible possess and impress you. The Bible is inspired; even if it is left unread and allowed to collect dust, it is still the Word of God. But that inspiration does not automatically affect you. God has spoken through men of old who wrote our Bible. Now it is your responsibility to find out *what* God communicated. You must read it prayerfully, with an open mind and an expecting heart. And if you actually discover what God says in His Word, you will be a changed person.

C. A Much Copied and Widely Read Communication

The Bible has been copied and quoted more times than any other book in human history. Of the Gospels alone there are over 1400 Greek manuscripts, about forty of which are over 1,000 years old. Of the entire Bible, no one knows exactly how many ancient manuscripts and fragments have been found. Just since 1947, eleven caves in the Dead Sea area have been discovered containing some complete scrolls (of Isaiah, for example), scroll portions, and thousands of Biblical fragments.[2] It will take scholars at least fifty years to put together and decipher all these Hebrew manuscripts. In addition to the Dead Sea finds, there have been unearthed many other ancient copies of the Bible in whole or in part.

In more modern times the Bible has been copied and preserved. The Vulgate (the Latin translation) was the first book published on the modern movable-type printing press. The book was called the Mazarin Bible and was done — at least so we think — in the town of

---

[2] In 1947 the "Dead Sea Scrolls" were found in a cave. Since 1947 a total of eleven caves have been discovered, thus exposing the thousands of Biblical fragments. No single fact about Bible discovery has been so thoroughly or frequently discussed recently. One of the best books on the subject is by the Yale professor, Millar Burrows, *The Dead Sea Scrolls* (New York: Viking Press, 1955). A popular, but trustworthy account of the finds is recorded in the *Reader's Digest* for April, 1956.

Mainz, Germany, in 1453. From the invention of the printing press to this day, the Bible has been printed literally millions of times. In fact, it has been printed more times than any other book; it has been translated in whole or in part into more than 1,200 languages, and missionaries are working hard and fast in many parts of the uncivilized world to get the Bible into still more languages. Moreover, the Bible sells more copies in the Western world every year by far and away than the top "best-seller."

Apparently God's Holy Spirit moves on the hearts of men to secure and read the Bible. Indeed, this is an obvious and very nearly universal fact. But why is the Bible, rather than some other book, chosen by the Holy Spirit for such wide circulation? The answer to that is the sheer content of the Biblical communication, and to that we give our attentions now.

II. THE CONTENT AND CHARACTER OF THE BIBLICAL COMMUNICATION

Time, space, and purpose do not permit us to outline here the content of the Scriptures in any detail. That exercise is reserved for our Bible classes in church and school. But it is highly important to point up the theme of the Bible and to observe, if briefly, the main content and character of the Biblical communication.

A. What Is Communicated?

The theme and purpose of the Bible is the redemption or salvation of man. Man sinned, says the Bible, causing the Fall or what John Milton, the poet, called the "first disobedience." (See Genesis 3.) This Fall or disobedience created a great gulf between God and man.

But God loved man so much that He bridged the gulf, thus making it possible for man and God to come back together and become friends all over again. Christ and Him crucified was that bridge to bring God and man back together (cf. John 3:16). The Old Testament leads up to the Christ of the New, and the whole Bible is the story of how God provided a way for man to get close to Him by preparing for and actually giving us Jesus Christ.

Now this is the most important story ever communicated, for it is the plan of salvation. This Biblical story tells us how we may have our sins forgiven, how to live the life of salvation, and how to have eternal life.

B. The Biblical Communication Is Authoritative

The Bible is not something to be taken or left at will, because it is the final court of appeal in matters of faith and conduct. No book in all of history makes so clear the content of doctrine and ethics.

Now this fact points up the simple truth that we must make the Bible our guidebook — more, our authoritative guidebook. When we go on a trip, we have a map or a guide. Life is a trip, and the Bible is our map or guidebook to heaven. A great Reformer asked, "How can I know the way to heaven?" "By reading the Bible," he answered.[3] The Bible was his only and authoritative

---

[3] The cults believe this too, but true Christians will weigh their interpretation and use of Scripture against a threefold authority: (1) Christ — what did He really teach? (2) the Bible — before jumping to a conclusion, look at the Bible as a whole to secure a full picture; (3) the Spirit — "Who conveys revelation, Who delegates its authority, and Who witnesses to its divinity." (Bernard Ramm, *The Pattern of Authority*. Grand Rapids: William B. Eerdmans Publishing Co., 1957, p. 36. Dr. Ramm gives a good statement on all three sources of authority.)

guide. David said, "Thy word is a lamp unto my feet, and a light unto my path" (Ps. 119:105). It must be ours too.

C. The Biblical Communication Is Obvious and Clear

Mark Twain once said facetiously what ought to be taken seriously. In a word, Twain said: "Not the parts of the Bible I don't understand, but the parts I do, bother me." Many a man has been unwilling to be so honest. Such unwilling people complain that the Bible is obscure, clouded, hidden in meaning, and therefore they claim to be in doubt about the general pattern of belief and moral behavior. But the truths of God in the Bible are repeated so often and in so many different ways — even in simple stories — that it is really quite impossible to miss the great arguments for salvation and love of neighbor. God himself said, "For the commandment which I command thee this day, it is not hidden from thee, neither is it far off" (Deut. 30:11).

To be sure, there are obscure passages in the Bible and commonly misinterpreted sections too. Of Paul's letters it is said that there are "some things hard to be understood." (II Peter 3:16). If there were no problems in Biblical interpretation, our Biblical scholars would be out of a job tomorrow. And it must be further said that, as earnest, intelligent Christians, we must seek continually to understand the Bible more completely. But who, if he is honest and is willing to read, can miss such important truths as these: that Christ can forgive sins, that man is a sinner who needs to be forgiven, that Christ died for his sins, that love of God and neighbor are tests of the forgiven, converted life. These great, eternal, and absolute truths are made clear in the Bible as they are nowhere else in literature and only a blind man can miss them.

NOTE ON TRANSLATIONS

New translations are needed periodically to keep pace with changing language patterns, thereby making the Word of God clear to each succeeding generation. The many translations of our own day have been exceedingly helpful in impressing God's Word on people young and old and of various walks and strata of society. Add that fact to this, that Biblical scholarship is constantly making strides in terms of unearthing new manuscripts and learning how better to translate God's Word. Thus we see the necessity of new translations.

Actually, translations (*versions*) of the Bible have been made throughout the centuries; this is no new idea. The Septuagint was completed long before Jesus Christ and was a translation of the Hebrew Scriptures into Greek because the mass of Greek-speaking Jews needed the Bible in their own language. The Egyptians had their own versions, too (the Sahidic, for example), and later Jerome translated the Bible into Latin and his version was known as the Vulgate. In modern times we have the Wycliffe version, the Tyndale and the King James versions, and the Revised Standard Version to mention only a few.

In more recent times a very large number of translations have been made into modern or popular English: Weymouth, Goodspeed, Moffatt, Way are but a few. Let us thank God for the insights and interest these translators have given to the reading and study of the Bible.

1. Scripture Readings

To be read: I Corinthians 2:6–13; II Timothy 3:10–17; Matthew 21:42–44; John 5:39; John 7:38; Acts 17:11; Acts 18:24, 28.

2. Bibliography

Gladstone, W. E. *The Impregnable Rock of Holy Scripture.* Philadelphia: John D. Wattles, 1891. Chapter 1.

Purkiser, W. T., Demaray, C. E., Metz, D. S., Stuneck, M. A. *Exploring the Old Testament.* Kansas City, Missouri: Beacon Hill Press, 1955. Chapter I.

Ramm, Bernard. *The Pattern of Authority.* Grand Rapids: William B. Eerdmans Publishing Co., 1957. Chapters 1, 2.

Smyth, J. Paterson. *How God Inspired the Bible.* New York: James Pott and Company, 1918. Especially chapters II and IV of Book I and chapter I of Book II.

3. Questions for Discussion

1. What does the word "Bible" mean?
2. What do we mean by revelation?
3. Wherein is the Holy Spirit an agent in Biblical communication?
4. Is the Bible an inspired book?
5. How do you account for the wide circulation the Bible enjoys?
6. Wherein is the Biblical communication authoritative?

5

Man and His Sin

A street sign pictures a preacher spreading butter on a piece of bread. In the advertisement, paid for by a leading butter distributor, the preacher is pictured as saying, "It's a sin to spread it thin." We smile at that, but it reflects the all-too-popular notion that sin, after all, is not very serious, and that it is something that may be taken lightly. It is the purpose of this chapter and the next to introduce us to the real nature of sin.

I. THE NATURE OF MAN

If we want to know what the real nature of sin is, we must first ask what man is. We may say that man is an animal because there are biological similarities between him and the other creatures of the world. But man is not merely an animal; he is the highest form of animal and is unique in the animal kingdom.

Why is man unique among the animals? Because, as we say in theology, he was created *Imago Dei,* that is, "in the image of God" (Gen. 1:26, 27). God is Spirit and Person; man is also spirit and person. Animals are neither spirits nor persons. Man, unlike the animals, is created in the image of the Spirit-Person God.

Now just what are the characteristics of this spirit-person animal called man? Some of the chief characteristics are listed below and each characteristic suggests the twofold truth that man is (1) to be distinguished from the other animals and (2) made in the image of God.

A. Man Is Self-reflective

Man, like God, has the capacity for self-reflection which other animals apparently do not have, at least, to any significant degree. This is to say that man can stand back, as it were, and look at himself; he can analyze his own acts and even his own thought processes. He can examine what he is, the world in which he finds himself, and what he does in his world. He can think about himself and evaluate his activities. Animals cannot do all these things.

B. Man Is Innately Religious

Man is born religious. Psychologists and theologians have known for a long time that men are born with the innate knowledge and feeling of need to serve and worship a higher being. William A. Spurrier in his *Guide to the Christian Faith* says, "Human nature is so constructed that we have to have a god. . . . That is why there are really few atheists in the world" (p. 75). Atheism is not native to man but is the product of man's sin; the knowledge of a supreme being is born in man. To be sure, the god people worship is not always the Christian God, but it is a god — power, success, money, or something else in which trust and hope can be placed.

C. Man Is Free

Man is free, but animals apparently do not possess freedom in the same sense man does. Man, like God, has

49

intelligence by which he controls himself and makes his decisions. Animals, if they possess any intelligence, possess a lower form of it, and therefore their freedom is limited. In theological terms, man is free to choose for or against God. Joshua said to the people of Israel, "Choose you this day whom ye will serve" (Josh. 24:15). This alternative does not confront the lower animal world. As Charles Kingsley said, "God made the animals to do each what it likes, without sin. But He made man to do more than what he *likes;* namely, to do what he *ought.*"

Man's freedom to choose for or against God is a highly significant fact. His choice determines for him a happy or miserable life here and hereafter. How often have we seen people use their freedom to reject God! And how often have we watched these people establish themselves in the ways of sin and therefore tragedy! But man can choose to go God's way; he can choose to establish patterns of righteous living. Not only can he choose to do so. It is his responsibility and duty to do so.

D.   Man Is a Sinner

A fourth characteristic of man is that he is a sinner. If man is free, he is free to do good or to sin; and he does sin. Every man knows the two opposing forces of his life, the one beckoning to God and righteousness, the other tempting to selfishness and sin. What is this selfishness we call sin, and what are the factors involved? We are now asking about the real nature of sin, and to that question we turn our attention.

II.   THE NATURE OF SIN

When man fell in the Garden of Eden, he did so because he wanted to put himself in the place of his

Creator. The creature wanted to think of himself as being greater than his Creator. He wanted to be independent of God. He wanted to control himself; he did not want God to control him. (Be sure to read the account of the Fall in Genesis 3.) This independent attitude or self-assertiveness we call pride. That one word pride is the most important word there is for an understanding of the real nature of sin. It was man's pride that made him reject God and get out of proper relatedness to God. It is God's desire that every man do His will. When man does not do His will, he transgresses (breaks) the law of God. This breaking of God's law is sin (cf. I John 3:4).

A. St. Augustine

It was St. Augustine in the fourth century, A.D., who established the simple truth that the nature of sin is pride. Isaiah (Isa. 9:9; 16:6) and Paul (I Tim. 3:6) and many others had stated this truth, but it did not seem to "sink in." But with Augustine this truth was made central in the Church's doctrine of sin. He was one of the greatest theologians who ever lived, and he continues to influence theology in our own day.

What do we mean when we say the nature of sin is pride? We mean that man commits no wrong which is not traceable to pride; to put it another way, every sin man commits is the product of a desire to protect the ego or self. Murder, adultery, stealing, falsifying, and any and every sin that man has ever committed or ever will commit is the result of pride. It was so with Adam and Eve. It has been so with every man since that time.

Perhaps this can best be illustrated by the following sketch.

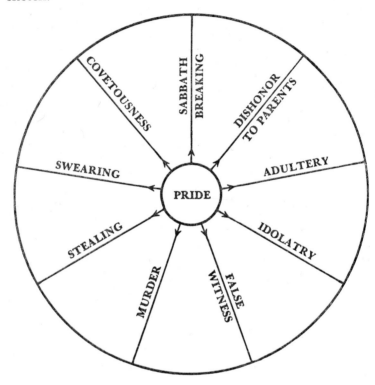

The major sins have been listed in the wheel above, and each one is pictured as being the product of pride, which is self-protection. It is an amazing fact that every sin does, in fact, issue from pride. If man commits adultery he does so to gratify self; he is doing what selfish desire dictates rather than respecting personality. If we covet we are aggravating the temptation to take what is not rightfully ours but something we imagine will make us happy. If we tell an untruth we are really "covering up" to prevent humiliation. We could go on through the rest of the sins, demonstrating that each is the product of sheer pride and the desire to protect the self.

B.   The Permanence of the *Imago Dei*

There is a very important point in analyzing the nature of sin and its reaction on the individual that must not be overlooked. That is this: the *Imago Dei* (image of God) is never completely destroyed. No matter how sinful a person may become, some of this image is left in him for he is still spirit and person, and the Spirit of God still moves on him. There are still possibilities in him. This is to say that the Image of God is born in man, and though it may become terribly marred by sin, it is never entirely taken from man. *The Imago Dei is a permanent gift of God.*

If this is true, then man never loses his capacity or freedom, nor his responsibility and duty, to choose for God. Let us take an analogy. Here is a young man who finds himself in prison. But whether he is in prison or at home, he is still the son of his father. He was born in the image of his father, he is the son of his father, and he has the capacity to choose to make amends and in time to return to the father's house even as the Prodigal did.

In all this, however, we must indicate a stern warning. There is the tragic force of habit. Very often people who find themselves in prison are so bound by the habit of sin that they cannot break the habit. Even after God has rescued them from their prison of sin, their old sinful habits and desires continue to plague them. *It is clear that we must encourage ourselves in the business of forming righteous habit patterns, patterns we do not need to break but want to keep.* (This, by the way, is why it is so important that parents be Christian and help their children to establish right habit patterns.)

Here we must refer to the miracle of conversion. God has entered the lives of many a hardened sinner. Yes, men who have been in prison and who were extremely wicked have been changed. God can break through that hard, thick wall of pride and expose the personality to the love of Deity, thereby making over the man. Conversion is perhaps best described in the prayer of Ephraim, "Turn thou me, and I shall be turned; for thou art the Lord my God" (Jer. 31:18). *In fact, the miracle of the gospel is that it has the capacity to make bad men good.*

C. The Tragic Effects of Sin

The tragic effects of sin will be noticed throughout these two chapters on sin; but here it is important to note that sin has its effects in two directions; it affects the individual himself, and it also affects others.

Thomas Lund tells the story of Leonardo da Vinci, finding real-life characters to pose for the famous "Last Supper," a painting done on the wall of a church in Milan, Italy. He found the perfect man for the central figure, Christ, a young man of remarkable personal charm and genuine character. During the months following, Da Vinci was able, too, to find men to pose for the other characters, with the single exception of "Judas." He could not locate such a man; Judas was difficult to find because he must be a man whose facial lines would give him away as a thief and a betrayer. After months of searching, Leonardo found his man. But when the sitting was completed, the young man broke down and wept. He said, "Two years ago I was the young man who sat for the central figure — the Christ. Since that time I have lived a life of sin and it has brought me now to the place where I can be the Judas in this picture."

It is one thing to be a Judas in this life — that is bad enough. But sin has its eternal implications too. Sin alienates the sinner from God and, if persisted in, results in eternal separation from God. This we might call the "eternal tragedy" of sin.

Yes, sin affects the individual himself!

Sin also affects others. As a matter of fact, you probably cannot think of a single sin that does not affect others. When one sins it is like throwing a pebble into a pool; the ripples radiate from the spot where the pebble landed. In like manner, when we sin the ripples of influence radiate to others from the bad act. The power of influence is something beyond the capacity for measurement. Of course, the way to influence for good is by loving people, for love is the opposite of sin. If we truly love, we cannot help but do good. Clarice Bowman, teacher of religious education at High Point College in North Carolina, observes: "Astounding researches by sociologists and cultural anthropologists reveal that the power of love has a chain reaction that goes on across the world, across the years. It makes differences in direct proportion to the selflessness of it." Why not throw your influence on the side of love rather than on the side of sin?

Carlyle once wrote that, "No other man has in him the divine rage against iniquity, falsity, and baseness that Ruskin has . . . ." Ruskin's gift for seeing into the real nature of sin was vividly expressed when he observed the effects of sin on others. In Venice, Ruskin saw a beautiful structure in ruins and said, "Someone has been untruthful, somebody has placed lying stones in these walls and foundations." Upon entering a home, he found people burning with fever and announced, "Someone put lying lead in the drainage pipes." Seeing a ship dashed to pieces and a hundred lives lost, Ruskin cried, "Someone has been untruthful. Somebody put lying links into the great cables of the anchor chain that ought to have held the ship when the storm came." Hurrying into a lovely church in a rainstorm, he noticed large buckets placed to catch water as it dripped from the magnificent fresco paintings of Tintoretto, on the ceiling, and said, "Somebody has been untruthful; somebody has placed lying tiles on the roof."

There you have it! Sin affects others. Never forget that; and never forget that it will affect you too.

1. Scripture Readings

To be read: Romans 5:6–11; Ephesians 2:1–10; I John 1:5–10; I John 2:1–6; Ezekiel 18:20–22, 30–32.

2. Bibliography

Lewis, C. S. *Mere Christianity*. Glasgow: William Collins Sons and Company, Ltd., 1955 (a Fontana Book). Book III, chapter 8.

Moule, H. C. G. *Outlines of Christian Doctrine*. London: Hodder and Stoughton, 1892. Chapter VIII.

Whale, J. S., *Christian Doctrine*. New York: Macmillan, 1941. Chapter II.

3. Questions for Discussion

1. What is the *Imago Dei*? Is it permanent? If so, wherein?
2. What are the characteristics that distinguish man from animals?
3. Describe St. Augustine's view of sin?
4. What can you say about the effects of sin?

6

Optimism Versus Pessimism

Now we must introduce ourselves to three views of man. The first is the optimistic belief that man is basically good and that he can bring to pass a good world by rolling up his sleeves and going at it. It says man in himself and by himself can make a good world. The second view is just the opposite: that man has no good in him, that he is helpless and must remain helpless when it comes to building a good world. This pessimistic view says man can never make a happy world. There is a third view which disagrees with both the optimistic and pessimistic views of man. It believes man is neither *all* good nor *all* bad. It holds a position between the two: man himself is both good and bad. Most important of all, it brings in a third factor. It holds that, by the help of God, man can do much good. In fact, man was created to be and do good.

Let us look at these three doctrines more closely.

I. THE OPTIMISTIC VIEW OF MAN

The first view is the most common and most popular and is believed even today. It is the idea that man is essentially good, that he is getting better and better, and that someday he will find himself living in a perfect world because he himself has made his world perfect. This idea, however, is somewhat out of date. Why is it out of date? The most obvious answer is that in our own day we have experienced two world wars. Man has tried to produce peace, but it is obvious that he is, in himself, incapable of doing that. Man is corrupt; he is a sinner. "All have sinned" (Rom. 3:23). Not only the New Testament but the experience of the race makes this clear.

Those who are so optimistic about man say that sin is ignorance. Ignorance, in turn, produces a defective environment, an environment in which it is both easy and natural to sin. Another way of putting it is that man is now going through a mere stage in the racial history, a stage which is analagous to adolescence. Once we have conquered ignorance and adolescence by education and maturity, man will quit making mistakes and sin will cease to exist.

What are we to say to this doctrine? Let us examine it and see.

A.   Man's Will Is Inadequate

No sheer act of the will can make a man better. I have been told that the man who said daily, "I am getting better and better every day in every way," died of suicide. Now this may be an apocryphal tale, but the point is obvious and true. Man cannot, in himself, make himself good, no matter how hard he tries. Job said it this way, "What is man, that he should be clean? and he which is born of a woman, that he should be righteous" (Job 15:14). Sooner or later he will discover himself inadequate to cope with his own sin; only God can take care of that.

The inadequacy of man's will, then, is a strike against this optimistic doctrine.

B.   Man's Knowledge Is Inadequate

It was Socrates who said that to *know* is to *do*. By that is meant that if one knows right from wrong he will always do the right. Obviously, Socrates had a great deal of faith in human nature. But he was mistaken. How often has the world known what to do but found itself incapable of doing it! Let us make it more personal; not a single person reading these lines can say that when he has known right from wrong he has *always* done the right. Too often we are like Paul, who said, "The good that I would, I do not; but the evil that I would not, that I do" (Rom. 7:19). The point is just this: knowledge is not enough; it takes more than knowledge to do the right. Contrary to the claim of these optimists, sin is more than mere ignorance.

C.   Man's Nature Is Warped

The third point follows naturally from the second. If the cause of sin is not mere ignorance, what is its cause? Man's nature is warped; there is something fundamentally wrong at the core of his personality. It is a mistake to assume that human nature is good. Human nature is not good; it is twisted; it is out of gear with things; it tends to run at cross purposes with the Law of God. Man's tendency is to sin; it is easier to do the wrong than to do the right. The essential thrust of human nature is toward the bad rather than toward the good.

Now this is no mere notion; this is fact. The fact is that men who know better, sin; and they sin because there is something fundamentally wrong with them. By nature they are evil. We are "by nature the children of wrath" (Eph. 2:3).

D. The New Testament and History versus This Optimism

This optimistic view of man teaches inevitable progress. But nowhere does the Bible promise inevitable progress. As a matter of fact, it makes clear that there will be no real progress when it says that there will always be "wars and rumors of wars" (Matt. 24:6). Furthermore, history gives no support to the idea of human progress. Someone has figured the amount of time in the history of the race that peace has existed all over the world at the same time. Comparatively speaking, it is nil! During almost every hour of civilization up to this point there has been organized fighting going on somewhere in the world. And if you want to bring matters down to individual situations, murders and crimes of every sort are committed constantly and have been through the centuries.

But someone says, "Surely civilization at the moment is at its best. Does it not look as if, with all our modern science and information, we have at last found the key to happiness and peace?" Unfortunately, the answer is "No." Even at this moment in history there are few real signs of progress. The H bomb is certainly no sign of hope; it is a terrifying instrument at sinful man's disposal. Moreover, one cannot help but wonder if the whole new system of rockets and satellites will not prove to be even more terrifying. The fact is that, were it not for the grace of God, the world already would have seen an Atomic war. It is only because of a longsuffering and merciful God that we "are not consumed" (Mal. 3:6).

History, past or present, then, cannot demonstrate that man is getting better. If after all these hundreds of years man has not demonstrated any real ability to usher in the Messianic age, how can we hope to do it in the future? The New Testament answer is that man of himself cannot hope to do this, because there is something fundamentally wrong with man inside. All are "under sin. . . . There is none righteous, no not one" (Rom. 3:9, 10). *With God, however, a better world can be made. The answer is in God, not man.*

E.   The Optimistic View and Pride

We come now to the most subtle difficulty with this high opinion of man. We have already established that the nature of sin is pride. What happens when a man gets to thinking he is perfectly good? Well, of course, he gets proud; and once he is proud, he sins. We have already seen why pride is sin and we need not review that here; but we do need to underscore this simple truth that to believe one "has arrived" is to sin. As soon as one becomes proud of his goodness, he sins, for pride itself is the nature of sin. But what about the man we regard as truly good? Ah! he himself is never quite sure he is good enough. It is this humility which is perhaps the most important characteristic of a converted person. The New Testament issues a solemn warning along this line when it declares that we must take care lest any of us think more highly of ourselves than we ought to think (Rom. 12:3).

Now we are ready to make a conclusion on this first view of man. We cannot accept this optimistic view of man, because evil is everywhere present as a result of man's evil propensities. There have always been and there always will be wars, murders, and crimes of every sort. Pick up today's or any day's newspaper; you will find it filled with fighting, crime, the struggle against war. We cannot, then, possibly believe that man, in himself, can be good or can produce a perfect world when we see all this sin about us.

There is, in fact, only one possibility for a good world; it is that all men should turn to Christ. Why? Because it is only through Christ working in us that we can accomplish any good (John 15:5).

II. The Pessimistic and Realistic Views of Man

It has been demonstrated that we cannot accept the doctrine of unbounded faith in man. It is also true that we cannot accept the doctrine of wholesale pessimism. It is no more Christian to be thoroughly pessimistic about man than that it is to be thoroughly optimistic about him. Complete despair is pagan, for the primitive peoples of the world have always looked at man as a poor, pathetic, hopeless creature. Pessimism says that under no circumstances can man do anything to make either himself or his world better; he is absolutely helpless, and no one or nothing can alter this hopeless situation.

First of all let us ask the question: "Is man himself totally corrupt?" The answer is *"Yes"* and *"No."* If men were totally corrupt and always followed their evil inclinations, life on this earth would be unbearable. If, on the other hand, we say man is not corrupt, we imply that man is good enough to help himself. But the truth lies not in one or the other, but in both. Man is corrupt but not as corrupt as he might be. Wherein is this position acceptable?

A.   Man Possesses Goodness

It is clear that man is born possessing a measure of goodness. Look into the eyes of a sweet little child. Who can say this precious possession is through and through evil, sinful, corrupt? There is about this little child something pure, good, and wholesome. That is why Jesus said we must become like little children (cf. Mark 10:15). Even after a child grows up, there is what we call the "milk of human kindness." He will be giving a helping hand to his neighbors and he will be showing kindness to many. Further, it is a strange but true fact that the milk of human kindness is not lost even on "skid row." A recent book about the world of tramps and drunks makes this clear. The author says that even the drunks on Third Avenue in New York City find themselves being kind in their own way to their fellow man.

B.   The Other Side of the Coin

If the above is true, we must conclude that man is not totally bad. But this is only half the answer or one side of the coin. When we turn the coin over, we see that in a very real sense man *is* totally corrupt. Why? Because sin extends to every dimension of human experience; sin permeates every province of behavior. Paul speaks of the law of sin which is in his members (Rom. 7:23), and says that without the power of God he can do no good nor save himself from sin. It is difficult if not impossible to think of a single act not tainted with sin. Even acts essentially good are done with mixed motives, as for example when we compliment a person because we hope to get a compliment or something we want in return. In fact, any good thing we do is always less than absolutely perfect. Isaiah said that "all our righteousnesses are as filthy rags" (Isa. 64:6). This fact — that sin finds its way into every range of activity — is what we mean by total depravity or the doctrine of total corruption.

Summary

Is man totally corrupt? Yes and No. There are two sides to the coin. One side tells us No, for goodness is seen in the little baby as well as in all adults. The other side of the coin says Yes, for we know that sooner or later this little child, so innocent in appearance now, will sin. The Scriptures bear this out by the candid remark, "All have sinned and come short . . . " (Rom. 3:23).

All this points up and summarizes the attitude of *realism*. Man is a sinner; that is a fact proved by experience and observation and taught by the Bible. It is only *realistic* to admit that fact. But man is also capable, under God, of being good. He was made in the image of God and has therefore, by God's grace, potential for righteous behavior.

1. Scripture Readings

To be read: Romans 5:12–14, 19; Psalm 51:1–5.

2. Bibliography

Moule, H. C. G. *Outlines of Christian Doctrine*. London: Hodder and Stoughton, 1892. Chapter VIII.

Whale, J. S. *Christian Doctrine*. New York: Macmillan, 1941. Chapter II.

Wiley, H. Orton. *Christian Theology*. Kansas City, Mo.: The Beacon Hill Press, 1941. Vol. II, chapter XIX.

3. Questions for Discussion

1. Distinguish and define: optimism, pessimism, realism.
2. What is meant when we say that man's nature is warped?
3. Wherein are the New Testament and history opposed to optimism?
4. What is the relation of optimism and pride?

7

Who Is Jesus Christ?

Jesus Christ was, of course, the founder of our Christian religion, just as Mohammed was the founder of Islam. But Jesus Christ was much different than Mohammed, and He was even more than the founder of the world's greatest religion. He was the promised Messiah, the Savior of the world; He was and is the Lord and Head of the Church. He was born of a Virgin[1] and was God incarnated in human flesh.

I. THE NAMES

"Jesus" is really the Greek form and equivalent of the Hebrew "Joshua." ("Isaiah" and "Hosea" are other forms of the same Hebrew name.) The Hebrew "Joshua" means "Jehovah is salvation." "Jesus" is the personal name of our Lord in the Gospels and Acts; in the Epistles it is combined with "Christ" or some other term.

"Christ" is the Greek equivalent of the Hebrew "Messiah" and means "the anointed one." "Jesus the

---

[1] See Edwin Lewis, *A Philosophy of the Christian Revelation*, chapter XIV, for a first class treatment of the Virgin Birth. Dr. Lewis accepts the Virgin Birth.

Christ" is a title for our Lord which means that He was the fulfiller of the Old Testament Messianic hope and prophecies (Isaiah 7:14; 11:1, 2; 42:1, 7; 49:6; 53; 61:1-3; Micah 5:2; Zechariah 9:9-10; 11:12-13; 12:10; 13:1, 6, 7; 14:2, 4). After the Resurrection, "Christ" was the frequent title given our Lord, because the Resurrection was a proof in the minds of the people that this Jesus was in fact the Messiah. Thus in the Epistles He is called most frequently "Jesus Christ" and sometimes just "Christ," which came to be used as a proper name.

Sometimes He is known as "the Lord Jesus Christ" or "our Lord Jesus Christ." The term "Lord" suggests His authority, headship, or mastery over us, His children. (In the first century and ancient times, slaves called their masters "Lord.")

II. JESUS WAS MAN

Jesus was a man. He was a real human being just as you and I are. Hebrews 2:17 reads, "Therefore he had to be made like his brethren in every respect, so that he might become a merciful and faithful high priest in the service of God, to make expiation for the sins of the people." Hebrews 4:15 serves to re-emphasize the truth that Jesus was human: "For we have not a high priest who is unable to sympathize with our weaknesses, but one who in every respect has been tempted as we are, yet without sinning" (R.S.V.). J. B. Phillips translates this last verse as follows: "For we have no superhuman High Priest to whom our weaknesses are unintelligible — He Himself has shared fully in all our experience of temptation, except that He never sinned."

The above quotations exemplify and make clear the

New Testament teaching that Jesus was a man. Tur-
genev has expressed the manhood of the Master by saying
that He had a "face like all men's faces." Yes, Jesus was
real; He existed in history; He was in actuality a human
being made of flesh and blood.

A. The Temptation to Heresy

It is easy to put too much emphasis on the deity or
divinity of Jesus Christ. In rebellion against liberalism,
the Church has often gone too far the other way and
sometimes it has found itself in the embarrassing position of emphasizing the deity of the Savior very nearly
to the exclusion of His humanity. Let this fact be made
clear: It is just as much a heresy to deny or under-em-
phasize the humanity of Jesus Christ as it is to minimize
His deity. At the moment in the theological world the
trend is toward the historical position that Jesus Christ
was equally human and divine.

In the second century A.D. the Gnostics reached the
summit of their influence. The Gnostics were heretics
and threatened the very survival of true Christianity.
They claimed to be Christians after a sort. They said,
among other things, that Jesus was not made of real flesh
and blood, that He just "appeared" to be real. They said
He was a mere phantom, and this phantom was called a
"Docetic" Christ. The Gnostics embraced this teaching
because of their belief that matter was evil.

Few people today would go so far as the Gnostics
did. How ridiculous to suggest that Jesus just "seemed"
to exist in the flesh! But that ancient Gnostic heresy has
left its mark on us. We often find it easier to think of
Christ as divine than to think of Him as human, not
because we think for a moment that He was unreal, but

because we are fearful of obscuring His deity. We still feel the impact of Gnosticism, giving us a nudge in the direction of de-emphasizing His humanity. But we must not yield to the temptation of heresy. Jesus Christ was equally God and man.

B. Jesus' Humanity and the Gospel Record

The Gospel record makes clear the humanity of Jesus. We read that He ate and drank and that He was hungry. He was tempted to sin, but, of course, He was without sin. Now the Gospels make clear that Jesus was thirsty, hungry, tired, tempted, etc., to let us know that He was a real man. But why is this so important? It is because the manhood of Jesus puts Him on our level. He knew suffering, temptation, and weariness just as you and I do, and therefore He can understand and sympathize with us. We have the comfort that our ascended Lord knows what we are like and takes our petitions and needs to the Father with genuine sympathy.

III. Jesus Christ Was God

In this human Jesus we have the revelation of God. "God was in Christ," St. Paul cried (II Cor. 5:19). He made reference to the Incarnation, and it is a miracle! It is absolutely unique, for it happened only once in all history and will never happen again.

Jesus Christ was more than a great religious leader such as Buddha, Zoroaster or Mohammed. He was more than a great philosopher such as Heraclitus, Plato, or Socrates. He was, in fact, God Himself, though a man.

A. Jesus' Knowledge of Himself

Some scholars, notably Albert Schweitzer, have said

that Jesus Christ did not know — or at best He imagined — that He was the divine Son of God, the Messiah. Other thinkers have suggested that He was not aware of His divine status until His Baptism, for He did not become divine until then.

All such theories reflect a mistaken idea of Jesus Christ, for He knew, and always knew, very well that He was more than a mere man. He was fully aware that He was God and the promised Messiah. "I and the Father are one" (John 10:30), He said repeatedly. Even as a child in the Temple — long before the Baptism — He said, "I must be about my Father's business" (Luke 2:49). "I came that they might have life, and have it abundantly" (John 10:10), He once said, clearly revealing his knowledge of His own Messianic role.

B.   The God-Man

What do we mean by the term, "Incarnate Christ"? We mean that the Son of man united with the Son of God to make the God-man. Thus He was "truly God and truly man."[2] He was both God and man and He was equally God and man.

This is a mystery too deep for the human mind to fathom. It is accepted by faith and on the basis of the Gospel record. Now the Gospel record makes clear at least four claims of Jesus which demonstrate the truth that He was the God-man. What are these four claims?

(1)   First, Jesus Christ claimed to have power to perform *supernatural acts*. These acts the New Testament calls "signs" or "miracles." When Jesus walked on the water, when He calmed the sea, when He healed

---

[2] From the definition of the Council of Chalcedon, A.D. 451.

blind Bartimaeus, He demonstrated His capacity to do the supernatural. When the Jews demanded that Jesus tell them plainly whether He was the Christ, He said, "The works that I do in my Father's name, they bear witness of me" (John 10:25).

(2) Then, Jesus had *unique moral insight*. He put into religion a new moral law, the Law of Love. This constituted a new dimension in religion; it was something beyond the Ten Commandments. It was conceivable that the Ten Commandments could be kept *without* loving one's neighbor. The Pharisees kept the Commandments, but the spirit of Love was not there. "A new commandment I give unto you, That ye love one another; as I have loved you, that ye also love one another" (John 13:34). Said Jesus in effect, "If one loves the Lord and his fellows wholeheartedly, he has not only kept the Mosaic Law but the Higher Law as well."

(3) Jesus claimed that He could *save from sin*. He forgave sin and in so doing released men from the power of sin and guilt feelings. This was the core of His message, which is summed up in John 3:16, "For God so loved the world, that he gave his only begotten Son, that whosoever believeth in him should not perish, but have everlasting life." Jesus was and is Savior and therefore can bring salvation. In fact, He himself is salvation, for He is Messiah.

(4) Finally, Jesus claimed *oneness with the Father*. Repeatedly we are confronted with Jesus' statement (found especially in John) that, "I and the Father are one." To know the Father is to know Christ; to know Christ is to know the Father (cf. John 14:7). The Father sent the Christ and the Father has control over Him; but

He and the Father are one, just as a beam of light and the light itself are one.

C.   The Uniqueness of the God-Man

We have before us four claims of Jesus: His miracles, His moral insights, His salvation, His oneness with the Father. These point up the uniqueness of His character and demonstrate the fact of the Incarnation. No other man can honestly make these claims. To be sure, many have claimed to be miracle-workers; but are they? If any miracles are accomplished, the credit must go, not to a mere man (who is but the instrument of God), but to supernatural forces. Unlike Jesus, no man has power within himself to perform miracles. Or take the claim to moral insights. Many a philosopher before Jesus came close to the Law of Love; but no one was able to define and clarify it with the same authority. Nor has anyone in history illustrated it by personal living as did Jesus of Nazareth. Then there is the claim to save from sin. No one — and many have claimed this power — but Jesus can save from sin. The Scriptures make this clear by the question, "Who can forgive sin but God alone?" (Mark 2:7). The final claim has to do with the oneness of God and Christ. Many a mystic has attempted to "lose himself in God," and some have, no doubt, had great experiences. But how complete and how consistent has this "oneness" of experience proved to be? Any honest Christian, however saintly, would readily admit that his experience of "oneness" with God has been wretchedly incomplete and woefully spasmodic.

So it is that Jesus Christ is the only person in history who can honestly make the claims of being the God-man.

There is another argument for the uniqueness of

71

Jesus which also points up the fact of the Incarnation and which should be observed here. This is the fact that He was the only man who ever lived who did not sin. It was noted above that Jesus was morally perfect; it was noted also that He was tempted to sin; but it is made clear in the New Testament that Jesus Christ did not sin. Concerning Him Peter testified that He "did no sin, neither was guile found in his mouth" (I Peter 2:22). Even in His severe crisis experience during the Temptation when He was hungry, when He was lonely, when He was dejected, when all the forces of psychic depression bore in upon Him — in the midst of all this, He did not sin.

Is there another man in history who can really make this claim? No. This is but another proof that Jesus Christ was the Incarnate Son of God.

Summary

Who is Jesus Christ? He is both man and God. He came to show us what God is like. He is Savior; He is Master; He is the Wonder Worker, performing the mighty acts of God; He is the Author of Love; He is unique; He is God Incarnate.

1. Scripture Readings

To be read: Hebrews 2:14–18; 4:14–16; John 1:1–18; 5:17–18; 5:25–27; chapter 9.

2. Bibliography

Berkhof, Louis. *Manual of Christian Doctrine*. Grand Rapids: Eerdmans, 1953, pp. 175–199.

Baillie, D. M. *God Was in Christ*. New York: Scribner's, 1955.

Moule, H. C. G. *Outlines of Christian Doctrine*. Chapters IV, V.

Warfield, B. B. *The Lord of Glory*. Grand Rapids: Zondervan, n. d.

Whale, J. S. *Christian Doctrine*. Chapter V.

Wiley, H. Orton. *Christian Theology*. Vol. II, chapters **XX**, **XXI**, **XXII**.

3. Questions for Discussion

1. Can you give scriptural support for the manhood and deity of Jesus Christ?
2. What does the term "Incarnation" mean?
3. What four major claims did Jesus make which suggest the truth that He was the God-man?

8

Jesus Christ and His Church

The New Testament word for church is EKKLE-SIA. This Greek word literally means "a calling out" from the world; thus, those belonging to the Church are God's "chosen" ones or His "elect." EKKLESIA came to mean an "assembly," or "congregation," also "community"; and these are, of course, the concepts that come to mind when we refer to the Church.

I. JESUS THE FOUNDER OF THE CHURCH

Jesus came to earth to found the Church[1] (see Matthew 16:18). His life, death, and resurrection were all aimed at founding the Church. This aim was accomplished, for Pentecost (Acts 2) was the birthday of the Church, and the Church is with us to this day in great strength.

But when we say that Jesus came to found the Church, we mean by the Church not just a building or even an organization. We mean those things, but by the Church we also mean something much deeper. Now it

---

[1] See John Wick Bowman, *The Intention of Jesus* (Philadelphia: The Westminster Press, 1943).

is this "something much deeper" which constitutes the essence of the Church.

A.   The Church Is the Family of God

Jesus instructed us to call God "our father," and He told us that we can be sons of God. It is this Father-son relationship which points up the true meaning of the Church which Jesus founded. The Church is the family of God because all those in it are God's children and God is their Father.

Now Jesus came to make possible this Father-son relationship. First He showed us what the relationship was like, for He Himself was a Son and He called God His Father. He was an example of a perfect Church member. He obeyed the Father because He loved Him and was fully dedicated to Him. In like manner, if we are to be true sons of God, we must love, serve, and obey the Father.

Jesus, however, was more than a perfect example. He was the Teacher of the Faith; He laid down the principles of belief and practice which one must follow if one wishes to be a member of the Father's family. The core of Christ's teaching was *love,* love of God and man. Matthew records these words: "Jesus said, Thou shalt love the Lord thy God with all thy heart, and with all thy soul, and with all thy mind. This is the first and great commandment. And the second is like unto it, Thou shalt love thy neighbor as thyself" (22:37–39). Now, if one really loves God, and his fellow man as much as himself, he is a member of the Family of God, which is the Church. He has been born again and has the promise of eternal life.

75

B. The Resurrection

Jesus' teachings all sounded very good to the disciples and other followers, and they never ceased to be amazed at His behavior, which exemplified beautifully what He taught. But this was not enough to found and establish the church. Christ must die and come forth from the grave victorious before the Church could be established.

When Christ went to the cross, the disciples doubted that Jesus was really their Messiah (Luke 24:21). They did not seem to realize that the cross was part of God's plan. Having given up hope in Christ and the movement He had started, the disciples even went back to fishing. But in the midst of their disappointment something extraordinary happened: Christ arose! He arose victor over death and the grave, proving to the amazed disciples that He was in fact the Messiah, the answer to their hopes and dreams. The disciples were so excited over the Resurrection that they could not cease speaking about it. The Resurrection clenched for them the truth that Christ was their Messiah, their Leader, and the Founder of the Faith they would now embrace.

After the Resurrection, Christ walked and talked with the disciples and the people who companied with them. On one occasion He was seen by more than "five hundred brethren at once" (I Corinthians 15:6). Now the movement began to grow because people were persuaded by the fact of the Resurrection. "This," reasoned the people, "could not have happened without God; this movement is therefore sound; we will follow this Teacher come from God."

76

C.   The Birthday of the Christian Church

The Resurrection of Christ, then, gave the real impetus to the Christian movement. But the Church was still not founded.

Christ, after the Resurrection, stayed with His friends on earth some forty days, long enough to establish firmly that He was no "phony," but actually resurrected and therefore the true representative of God. Then He told His disciples a very important thing — He said He would leave them and go back to His Father in heaven, and that they would have to take over His work on earth. He made it clear that they must tell everyone — even to the ends of the earth — the story of Christ and His resurrection. In this way they would secure the loyalties of many more people. Now Christ knew very well that the disciples and their helpers could not do this in their own strength, so He promised them that after His ascension the Holy Spirit would come to help them. He told them to wait in Jerusalem for the coming of the Holy Spirit. Read in this connection Mark 16:14–20; Luke 24:44–53; Acts 1:1–9.

On the Day of Pentecost,[2] the disciples and other followers of Christ were "altogether in one place" (Acts 2:1). They waited reverently and in much prayer for the promised Spirit. Suddenly He came "like the rush of a mighty wind, and it filled all the house where they were sitting. And there appeared to them tongues as of fire, distributed and resting on each one of them. And they were all filled with the Holy Spirit and began to speak

[2] Pentecost was a Jewish festival day taking place fifty *(pentekonta)* days after the Passover.

in other tongues as the Spirit gave them utterance" (Acts 2:2-4).

When all this took place there were, in Jerusalem, Jews from "every nation under heaven." These Jews were there to celebrate a great festival called Pentecost. When they witnessed the expression of the Spirit and heard the people speaking, they began to gather to see what the event was. As they got closer, they could hear what they said, and what was amazing was that these Jews from "every nation" understood, each in his own language. Some made fun of the Spirit-filled people, and others said they were drunk. But Peter rose to the occasion and explained that these were not drunk men, but Spirit-possessed men. He told them about Jesus and how the Jews had caused His death but how He had risen from the dead. Now the people listened more carefully, for they realized that they were in the presence of a strange and wonderful thing, that God was in this. Many — in fact about 3,000 — believed what Peter said, and they promised to follow his Christ. All this you can read in Acts 2.

Remember that these people came from all over the ancient world. That fact is important, for they took the Good News of Peter's sermon back to their own countries and paved the way for the establishment of many churches. Peter, John, and later Paul, Barnabas, and others went throughout Jerusalem, Judea, and to the "uttermost part of the world" telling the story of the resurrected Christ. This story was believed by thousands because the apostles were filled with the Holy Spirit, Who gave authority to their message. In this manner the

Church of Jesus Christ was born, became established, and grew.

II. JESUS CHRIST AND THE CHURCH'S UNITY

One of the most amazing characteristics of the new Church was its unity or oneness, or what we might call its "togetherness." How often those early chapters in Acts refer to this fact! Here are some typical statements: "They were all together in one place" (Acts 2:1); "And all that believed were together" (Acts 2:44); "Now the multitude of them that believed were of one heart and soul" (Acts 4:32). The Holy Spirit had so captivated the little group of Christians that their differences were lost in holy activity, and they were united in a single aim — to introduce the world to Jesus Christ.

It is in Jesus Christ that real Church unity consists. There is, in fact, no unity other than in Jesus Christ. Because of Jesus Christ, the Church is one in name, prayer, baptism, eucharist (the Lord's Supper), hymnody, redemption, etc. Any Church embracing the historic faith is called a *Christian* Church; it is a remarkable fact that our denominational differences are lost in prayer to God; converts are baptized into Christ, not into a denomination; all partake of the table of the Lord, not the table of a particular church group; all preach the one gospel, Christ crucified and resurrected; all sing of the same Christ; all are saved by the one redemption of the one crucified Lord.

John Wesley spoke of Christian hearts being "strangely knit together," an experience every true Christian knows. Have you not been on a bus or a train or in some strange place and found yourself talking with a perfect stranger, but a Christian? You do not know at first that he is a Christian, but it does not take long to find out. A word spoken, a behavior pattern revealed — something suggests that your partner in conversation is a Christian. You dare to ask if he is a Christian. "Why, yes," he replies. "And you — you are a Christian too!" Immediately the conversation takes on certain liveliness. You are no longer strangers. There is oneness between you. You sense the feeling of "togetherness," for the two of you are "strangely knit together." But why? Because you have something in common, something unspeakably wonderful, no ordinary possession. That possession is Jesus Christ. It is the Spirit of Jesus, the Holy Spirit, which knits you together and gives you both that incurable desire to bring others — the whole world if you could — into this fellowship the two of you enjoy so much.

A.   The Fellowship of Joy

This joy experienced by Christians in fellowship was characteristic of first-century Christians too. It has always been characteristic of true Christians. Persecution, famine, or peril do not take away the joy of the born-again person. There may be disappointment — that is inescapable — but there is an undertone of joy deep in the heart of every believer. This is the activity of God Himself in the individual's life.

B.   Christian Unity and the Joyful Heart

Now if this sense of joy is characteristic of all Christians, it must be one significant indication of unity. To discover Christ is an exciting business, and it brings joy. Jesus said the Kingdom is like a man who finds buried treasure. He is so excited over his discovery that he cannot keep quiet about it. The blood throbs and pulsates in his veins as he shouts, "I have found it!"

Christians have found a Treasure, something far better than buried treasure. That Treasure is Jesus Christ. He is the reason for the Christian's joy, for He gives peace in place of anxiety, love in place of hate, and purpose for living in place of confused aims. The Christian cannot keep still about his discovery of Christ; his every behavior pattern reveals his own inner joy; everyone knows he is the possessor of Treasure, a Person Who brings joy.

C. Unity in Mission

It is God's plan that the personal joy of a Christian be contagious, and it is. Who can be in the presence of happy Christians and not want to be part of this satisfying fellowship? And who can be part of the fellowship and have no desire to include the outsider in the fellowship of joy? The genius of gospel propagation is in the believer himself and in the fellowship itself; for in the believer and in the Christian group there is an experience and a way of life the world really wants.

True Christians tell others about this way of life; they help the unsaved discover their Christ; they introduce the outsider into the fellowship of the joyful heart. This is missionary activity, and the real Christians are unified in their desire to propagate this joyful way of life.

D. The Holy Spirit and Christian Unity

All through this chapter the Holy Spirit is mentioned. But just what is the Holy Spirit? And wherein is He the source of the Church's unity?

Sometimes we refer to the Holy Spirit as the Holy

Ghost. The old Anglo-Saxon word for ghost was *gast,* which meant "breath" or "spirit" or "soul." Actually, this comes very close to the original Hebrew and Greek meaning of *spirit.* The Hebrew word for spirit is *ruach,* which suggests "wind," and when applied to God's Spirit meant His activity and presence within people. Thus the Psalmist says, "Take not thy spirit (*ruach*) from me" (Psalms 51:11). Even as wind or air is breathed and serves a function *in* man, so the Spirit of God is in man, performing His holy function.

The Greek word for spirit is *pneuma* and also suggests the idea of "wind" or "air." (A pneumatic drill is an air drill; pneumatic tires are air-filled tires.) This invisible Spirit is within us, acting, powerful, real (Acts 1:8).

In the chapter on sanctification we will see that the Holy Spirit can fill us, thereby producing in us love and the other fruit of the Spirit, and the power to witness. Here we want to underscore the fact that the Holy Spirit binds Christians together in a unity of fellowship. Paul speaks of the "fellowship of the Holy Spirit" (II Corinthians 13:14). Here the Greek word for fellowship is *koinonia* and has the idea of community, "togetherness," unity. You may know of some church which has a *koinonia* Sunday school class or other group by that name. That is a most appropriate name for a church group, for Christians are truly bound together in the Spirit of God in Christ.

The Holy Spirit, the third person of the Trinity, is, then, invisible like the wind, but also like the wind, powerful. He can fill us with His presence and holy activity, causing us to love and serve. His presence in individuals produces *koinonia* (fellowship, community) in the Christian group which is the highest type of religious unity.

Summary on the Church's Unity

The Spirit binds individual Christians together in unity. He does this by providing a common center around which Christian lives are adjusted; Jesus Christ is that common center. In name, prayer, sacraments, gospel, hymnody, and redemption all Christians are unified, for all these are in the name of Christ. To discover the Christ is exciting and joyful; and the Church, the fellowship of joy, is united in the purpose of extending its borders. Joy and missionary activity go hand in hand and help demonstrate the unity of God's people. The Holy Spirit makes real the unity of God's people in the *koinonia* (fellowship).

1. Scripture Readings

To be read: I Corinthians chapter 15; Matthew chapter 28; Matthew 16:13-20; Acts chapter 2; 4:32-37.

2. Bibliography

Brunner, Emil. *Our Faith.* London: S. C. M. Press, Ltd., 1949. Chapter 28.

Hunter, A. M. *Interpreting the New Testament, 1900-1950.* London: S. C. M. Press, Ltd., 1951. Pp. 135-137.

Schmidt, Karl Ludwig. *The Church* (Bible Key Words from Gerhard Kittel's *Theologisches Worterbuch Zum Neuen Testament*). London: Adam and Charles Black, 1950. (For the advanced student.)

Whale, J. S. *Christian Doctrine.* Chapter VI.

Wiley, H. Orton. *Christian Theology.* Vol. III, chapters XXXI and XXXII (pp. 138-155).

3. Questions for Discussion

1. Why is the Church the family of God?

2. What is the relation of the resurrection of Jesus Christ to the founding of the Church?

3. What is the relation of the outpouring of the Spirit at Pentecost to the Church?

4. In what ways is the true Church unified? How do such factors as the Spirit, fellowship, joy, and mission figure into the Church's unity?

9

What Is the Atonement?

St. Paul said the cross was the very center of our faith and Christians since Paul have said the same thing. If the cross is so important, we must find out why it is and what it really means.

I. THE CROSS

In the first century the cross was a means of punishing a criminal by death, and it was the most painful method of public death at that. The people abhorred the thought of the cross, for they knew all too well about this gruesome method of punishment. Even the huge, burly soldiers could scarcely get accustomed to handling criminals in this manner, and often the soldiers numbed their senses with strong drink before an execution.

A. The Method of Crucifixion

Just how was a criminal crucified in the first century? In the first place, the victim was scourged, that is, whipped. This whipping was so severe that the victim often died under it. Jesus did not escape the scourging (John 19:1). Next it was customary for the crossbar to be bound on the victim's back, and sometimes he was forced to carry the whole cross as in the case of Jesus.[1] The criminal was now led through the streets by a centurion and four soldiers who had been commanded to do the execution. The title, put on whitened wood, was done in black letters and carried in front of the condemned man to announce to viewers why he was to die.

At the place of execution the victim was stripped, and by custom the clothes went to the soldiers. (In Jesus' case, His inner robe was not divided among the soldiers because it was seamless and therefore the more valuable if left in one piece. The soldiers cast lots for this robe, (John 19:23–24).

The two parts of the cross, the crossbar and the vertical part, were put together and the whole cross raised on ladders. Sometimes the cross was put together on the ground, the victim being stretched out upon it and bound to it. The hands were nailed to the cross, and sometimes the feet, as in Jesus' case. It is not hard to imagine the shrieks of pain that came from the victim's lips when the nails were driven into his flesh.

The title was fixed to the top of the cross and the criminal left to die. Dying in this manner was slow, the man lingering for hours or even days. Jesus was crucified at nine in the morning and died around three that afternoon (Mark 15:25, 34).

B. The Shame of the Cross

Crucifixion was the worst method of death known to the ancient Roman world. The pain was severe; in fact, it was excruciating. Says James Orr of the cross, "With

---

[1] Simon of Cyrene helped Jesus carry His cross (Mark 15:21; Matthew 27:32).

its prolonged and excruciating torture, it was the most agonizing and ignominious death which the cruelty of a cruel age could devise."[2] Every criminal prayed that a cross would not be his lot. The shame, too, made it the worst kind of death. The victim was naked and exposed to passersby who laughed and made sport of him. Jesus did not escape such mockery (Luke 23:35–37). The mockery, coupled with the fact that the cross was reserved for criminals, slaves, and foreigners, made for humiliation indeed.

So it was that the New Testament writers frequently referred to the shame of Jesus' death. Hebrews 12:2, for example, speaks of Jesus Who "endured the cross, despising the shame," and elsewhere Jesus is referred to as having been "accursed" or as being an "anathema."

The cross of Jesus Christ with all its shame and pain was the most tragic event in history, for He was the perfect Son of God. (He could hardly be classed as a criminal!) But let us see how God took this most tragic of events and made it into the most glorious event of history.

II. THE ATONEMENT

Every man knows that he has sinned, that he is estranged from God, and that he needs to find his way back to God. It is in this matter of finding one's way back to God that the essence of atonement is suggested. In fact, atonement has been defined as "the creation of conditions whereby God and man come together."[3]

---

[2] James Orr, "Jesus Christ," *International Standard Bible Encyclopedia*, III, 1662.

[3] J. S. Whale, *Christian Doctrine* (New York: The Macmillan Company, 1947), p. 75.

A. Man Cannot Make Atonement

The real problem of atonement is this: Who will create the conditions whereby God and man can come together?[4] Man himself cannot create these conditions. Christianity says the gospel begins at the cross and that in the cross the conditions were created whereby God and man can be brought together. The cross is God's, not man's act. Men were only the instruments of the execution of Jesus, but the cross itself was all part of the fulfillment of God the Father's plan.

Man cannot atone for his sins by gifts. Acts of charity are all very good, and anyone who is identified with the Kingdom-building enterprise knows very well that Christian institutions need sustaining funds. But such gifts, however great or small, though used for noble purposes, do not atone for our sins.

Furthermore, living a good life — even a very good one — will not atone for our sins. "I'm as good as the next fellow," we often hear, as if one's own goodness would secure him a place next to God. Some will even do a highly moral thing to attempt to bring themselves into contact with God. Perhaps the greatest temptation of the professional person who is in character-building work is the temptation to believe that he has done something so fine that he has helped atone for his sins. But this is not the teaching of the New Testament. The New Testament teaching is that one can do nothing to make atonement for sins; not even by doing wonderful things for the moral upbuilding of oneself and others can one atone for his sins.

---

[4] *Loc. cit.*

Still others have insisted that man can get close to God by self-abasement. Throughout history there have been those who have gone without food and clothing and who have even mistreated themselves with the idea that they are atoning for their own sins. The Hindu, who goes about half naked in the snow-covered Himalayas, is attempting to atone for his sins and free himself of guilt feelings. "Sin must be punished, therefore I will punish myself, a sinner," say these people. True, sin must be punished, but only God in Christ is capable of providing sufficient punishment.

B.   Only God Can Atone for Sin

It is very true that sin must be punished. This is a law of God that issues from His very nature, for righteousness cannot stand unrighteousness. If one breaks a law of the land, he is caught, tried and punished; if society did not operate this way, it would be so hectic it could not exist. The same is true of the spirit world; and God, in His love and wisdom and because of His justice, provided punishment and atonement for our sins. He sent His only Son, the Lamb of God, to die in our place and take on Himself the punishment due us (Isaiah 53:5; Hebrews 9:28; I Peter 2:24).

Atonement for sin, then, is solely the product of God's initiative and has nothing whatsoever to do with man's efforts. Thus Paul cries out for joy, "God was in Christ, reconciling the world unto Himself" (II Cor. 5:19). This is divine grace and love in action, and the Christ of the cross justifies man before the unbending righteousness of God.

C.   The Cross and Divine Forgiveness

In the Old Testament God taught that atonement

must be made for sin; thus animal sacrifices were a part of the Hebrew religion. These sacrifices pointed to the sacrifice of Christ. In the New Testament these animal sacrifices gave way to the sacrifice of the Christ Who died for sin once for all (Hebrews 7:27).

Also in the Old Testament age, God told His people that along with atonement for sin came forgiveness of sin (Leviticus 4:20; 5:10; etc.). By the same token in the New Testament age, Jesus Christ provides forgiveness through His atoning work on the cross. Thus, the meaning of atonement for the sinner is this: God, by His love, provided atonement for man's sin; and if the sinner repents, he is forgiven.

D.   The Cross and Divine Love

Now it cannot be too strongly emphasized that the cross was an act of *love*. Imagine you, a parent, allowing your son — your only son, who was innocent — to suffer and die in the place of a real criminal. This would indeed take a great deal of love on your part! But you are willing because you want to see the freedom of the criminal. By the same token "God so loved the world, that he gave his only Son . . . ," says John (3:16). It is no wonder John cried, "We love, because he first loved us" (I John 4:19).

In the eleventh and twelfth centuries there lived a remarkable monk, Bernard of Clairvaux. He possessed tender affection for his crucified Lord and had unusual insight into the love that sent the Savior to the cross, as expressed in his famous hymn, "O Sacred Head, Now Wounded":

> O sacred Head, now wounded,
>   With grief and shame weighed down,

Now scornfully surrounded
  With thorns, thine only crown!
O sacred Head, what glory,
  What bliss till now was thine!
Yet, though despised and gory,
  I joy to call thee mine.

What thou, my Lord, hast suffered
  Was all for sinners' gain:
Mine, mine was the transgression,
  But thine the deadly pain.
Lo, here I fall, my Saviour:
  'Tis I deserve thy place;
Look on me with thy favor,
  Vouchsafe to me thy grace.

What language shall I borrow,
  To thank thee, dearest Friend,
For this thy dying sorrow,
  Thy pity without end?
O make me thine forever;
  And should I fainting be,
Lord, let me never, never
  Outlive my love to thee.

Be near when I am dying,
  O show thy cross to me;
And for my succor flying,
  Come, Lord, and set me free.
These eyes, new faith receiving,
  From Jesus shall not move,
For he who dies believing
  Dies safely through thy love.

Summary

What do we mean by atonement? We mean that God, through His infinite love, created the conditions whereby God and man can come together. Man's sin offended the righteous God, but God Himself took the initiative in an act of reconciliation. The pain and shame of the cross help us to appreciate the effort of God in

Christ in providing atonement and reconciliation. The pain and shame of the cross further serve to accentuate God's love for us; the cross makes us want to love Him and repent of our sins.

The cross was the most tragic event in history, because wicked men killed the only Son of God, Who lived a perfect life. But God took this worst event and made it into the most blessed event in history, for the cross meant that man could be forgiven and enjoy eternal life.

1. Scripture Passages

To be read: John 12:27–28; John chapters 18, 19; Matthew chapters 26, 27.

2. Bibliography

Whale, J. S. *Christian Doctrine.* Chapter IV.
Wiley, H. Orton. *Christian Theology.* Vol. II, chapters XXIII, XXIV.

3. Questions for Discussion

1. Describe the method of crucifixion in ancient times.
2. Wherein was the cross shameful to the victim?
3. Why cannot man atone for his own sins?
4. What is the relation of the cross and forgiveness?
5. Why does the cross reveal love? Should it make us respond in love to God?

10

Repentance and Conversion

I. THE MEANING OF CONVERSION

In the Old Testament there are two Hebrew words for conversion, both of which convey the idea of repentance. In the New Testament there are three Greek words for conversion, and these also mean essentially "to repent." The teaching of Scripture, then, is this, that repentance leads to conversion.

A. Repentance

The word most frequently used for conversion in the New Testament is METANOEO. This word means literally, "I change my mind," or "I change the inner man." It further conveys the idea of turning around and going in the other direction. Before one is converted, he is traveling in the wrong direction on the road of life. He is heading for moral and spiritual destruction. But after conversion, he is going in precisely the opposite direction: he is heading for moral and spiritual well-being. The one direction on the road of life leads to disintegration, the opposite leads to integration; the one leads to maladjustment, the other to adjustment; the one to destruction, the other to construction; the one leads to evil and unhappiness, the other to righteousness and joy.

B. What Happens in Repentance?

It is one thing to say that repentance brings a changed life but quite another actually to repent. Now just what is involved in this repentance that brings conversion?

(1) The first factor in repentance is *recognition* — recognition of one's sinful way of life and of one's guilt. In one place Paul speaks of it as "knowledge of sin" (Rom. 3:20). It also means admission that one is helpless to save himself from sin and that he *needs* to be saved from sin. This is no easy step, for we are proud, independent creatures, and we do not like admitting we are sinners, nor do we like admitting that only Someone outside ourselves can free us from the bondage of sin.

(2) A second factor in repentance is *sorrow*. St. Paul refers to that "godly grief" which "produces a repentance that leads to salvation" (II Corinthians 7:10).

(3) The third factor has to do with a change of *purpose*. One's aim in life is quite different after he truly repents. It is the *will* at work here: the sinner now determines to turn around on the road of life and go in the other direction. Thus one has the disposition to turn from his sinful ways and to seek release from sin. Cf. Jer. 25:5.

Thus in repentance one *recognizes* his need, is *sorry* for his sins, and *purposes* in his heart to follow God. If it is possible to divide these three into psychological categories, we could say that recognition is an *intellectual* activity, that sorrow is an *emotional* reaction, and that purposing is essentially a *volitional* response.

It would be interesting and instructive to read in this connection David's Psalm of repentance (Ps. 51).

C. Faith and Repentance

One recognizes, sorrows, and purposes because of God's gift of faith. A spiritually blind man cannot "see" his need; an emotionally "cold" man toward God and righteousness cannot sorrow for his sins; a "hard" man cannot will to seek God. But God the Holy Spirit convicts of sin and offers faith for repentance.

Now faith is putting our trust in God; it is believing that He will hear our repentant plea and forgive us our sins and give us the salvation and inner peace we long for. Paul says that "being justified by faith, we have peace with God through our Lord Jesus Christ" (Rom. 5:1). Faith is the inward acceptance of God as real and trustworthy, and more — as beneficial and even obligatory (absolutely essential). Scripture tells us that "without faith it is impossible to please him [God]" (Heb. 11:6). In faith one recognizes spiritual verities and moral truth as of uttermost value.[1]

II. THE FACT OF CONVERSION

Conversion is a fact. It is not something imagined, nor is it a kind of self-induced experience which gives one a "good feeling." It may, it is true, produce in one a good feeling; but conversion itself is the result of a genuine, supernatural act of God; it is not merely an emotionally induced and momentary experience of release.

---

[1] Two kinds of faith are distinguished: *historical* faith, or belief in the Scriptures and orthodox traditions of the Church; and *saving* or *practical* faith, in which intellect, emotions, and will are operative in accepting God's offer of salvation through Christ.

A.   The Conversion Fact Illustrated from the Bible

In Acts chapter 9, we have the story of Saul's conversion. Saul was on his way to Damascus with the aim of persecuting Christians. But on his way to the city a great light shown out of heaven and blinded him. He fell to the ground and heard a voice which addressed him: "Saul, Saul, why do you persecute me?" This was Jesus Himself speaking. Jesus gave him instructions to go into the city, where Saul spent three days in blindness, after which a believer named Ananias touched his eyes so he could see.

This experience changed Saul completely. He stopped persecuting the Christians; indeed, he joined forces with the Christians and became a staunch follower of Jesus Christ and perhaps the greatest preacher the Christian Church has ever produced.

Here is no mere myth but the record of an actual event. Conversion was a fact, a reality, for St. Paul.

We could continue with the stories of Lydia "whose heart the Lord opened" (Acts 16:14), of the woman at the well (John 4), of the blind man in John 9, etc., demonstrating the *fact* of conversion from the Bible. There was obviously no doubt in the minds of the converted or in the minds of the Biblical writers; it was all conclusive; these people had met God and were transformed.

B.   The Conversion Fact Illustrated from History

The classic story of John Wesley's conversion will serve to illustrate the fact of conversion in history. It happened May 24, 1738. John Wesley, already an ordained man, was a member of a little group which met for prayer and Bible study in an apartment on Aldersgate

Street, London. On the night of May 24, John was not of a mind to go to the little meeting. Nonetheless, he went; and when he arrived late, one of the members was reading from the preface to Luther's commentary on the book of Romans. Then something happened! "About a quarter before nine," John Wesley wrote in his *Journal,* "while he [the reader] was describing the change which God works in the heart through faith in Christ, I felt my heart strangely warmed. I felt I did trust in Christ alone, for salvation; and an assurance was given me, that He had taken away my sins, even mine, and saved me from the law of sin and death."[2]

Not only does that simple statement have the ring of authority about it, but the fruits of John Wesley's conversion further serve to demonstrate that his was a genuine transformation. He went out to change England, for, as many a competent historian now says, John Wesley averted a revolution in England comparable to the revolution that actually took place in France.

Time and space do not permit recounting the conversion experience of Augustine, of John Newton, Francis Asbury, or of many another in evangelical history. But this much is true: thousands in every age since Jesus Christ have known by personal experience the astounding fact that, though once blind, they were made to see. God can take a bad man and make him good. This is not wishful thinking; this is fact.[3]

---

[2].John Wesley, *Journal,* May 24, 1738.

[3] It should be noted that many conversion experiences are not so climactic as Wesley's or Paul's. The important factor is not the *method* but the inner *knowledge* that one is a child of God.

III. KNOWLEDGE OF CONVERSION

How can I know that I am saved or converted? This is a question that has troubled many people. It is important that this problem be understood and its solution clarified.

A. The Temptation to Expect Universal Reactions

Because we are all quite different from one another, the experience of conversion produces differing reactions. Some react matter-of-factly, others almost hilariously. Some have scarcely any reaction at all, with little or no emotional response. Still others experience delayed reaction; this type surrenders his life to God but feels no different until some days, weeks, or even months have passed, after new habit patterns and new attitudes have been formed.

Now the temptation in all things is to expect universal reactions. This is true of conversion. We want everyone to respond just as we did at conversion. But God has not made us all to respond in the same way to conversion or any other experience. Even as all look different, so all respond differently. Some laugh heartily at hearing a humorous story, others just smile, and some only look pleasant. Some get very excited at an athletic event, others respond less overtly, and there are those who observe a game in their own quiet way. Difference in temperament and personality structure accounts for difference in reaction.

B. Feelings and Belief

Supposing a quiet-tempered person finds God in conversion. Should he expect to react with the same high feelings as a person of quite the opposite temperament?

Many persons have been troubled because they do not "feel" anything when they surrender to God. They expect that the New Birth will produce in them a sensation. So it may, but not necessarily. Others experience radical release from sin; the burden lifted, they feel relieved indeed. In a few days, however, the original feelings of release may have escaped them. This does not mean the believer has fallen out of fellowship with God; it simply means the initial excitement of conversion is over.

Here is a principle or law of spiritual existence: *Belief, not feelings, determines the validity of Christian experience.* If one believes that God in Christ is his Savior, and if one has in fact surrendered to the Savior, one's *feelings* have absolutely nothing to do with the *fact* of his conversion. C. S. Lewis phrases it this way, " . . . the great thing to remember is that, though our feelings come and go, His love for us does not."[4]

C. The Witness of the Spirit

If we depend on God's promise of salvation for personal knowledge of conversion, the inner witness of the Spirit will become a reality to us. " . . . The Spirit himself," says Paul, bears "witness with our spirit that we are children of God . . . " (Romans 8:16). This is one of the sure marks of a born-again person. There is an inner "knowledge" or "assurance" that the converted person is a child of God. There is a deep, settled peace,

---

[4] C. S. Lewis, *Mere Christianity* (Glasgow: William Collins Sons and Co., Ltd., 1955), p. 115.

the "peace that passes understanding." There emerges in the converted person the sense of well-being, or adjustment to God and one's fellows.

As one grows in the Christian way, the sense that he is living in the Spirit becomes increasingly clear. The fruit of the Spirit now begins to be in evidence: "Love, joy, peace, patience, kindness, goodness, gentleness, self-control" (Galatians 5:22–23). All this is the work of the Spirit and is evidence of His activity. If He is thus active, He "bears witness"; that is, He communicates or makes Himself real to the converted person.

John Wesley called this "assurance" of salvation, because the inner witness of the Spirit does, in fact, assure or convince us of conversion. We know, that is, we possess an inner conviction, wrought by experience, that God in Christ is our Savior.

1. Scriptural Passages

To be read: John 3:1–21; Acts 9:1–22; II Corinthians 7:8–11; John 16:8–11; Romans 8:12–17; 5:1–2; Galatians 5:16–25; Ephesians 2:1–10.

2. Bibliography

Demaray, Donald E., Editor. *Devotions and Prayers of John Wesley*. Grand Rapids: Baker Book House, 1957. Pp. 56–59.

Lewis, C. S. *Surprised by Joy, The Shape of My Early Life*. New York: Harcourt, Brace and Co., 1955.

————. *Mere Christianity*. Book III, chapters 7–9, 11–12.

Mackay, John A. *A Preface to Christian Theology*. New York: The Macmillan Co., 1941. Chapter 3.

3. Questions for Discussion

1. What does repentance really mean? What factors are involved?
2. What is the relation of faith and repentance?

3. Can you give illustrations of the conversion experience? What about your own conversion?
4. Discuss the temptation to expect universal reactions. Relate to the feeling or emotional factor in conversion.
5. What is the witness of the Spirit? What are the fruits of the Spirit?

11

What Is Sanctification?

Sanctification is a doctrine taught by Scripture, and it has been taught throughout the history of the Christian Church. Sometimes it has been taught incorrectly. It is our task in this chapter to make clear what sanctification[1] really means.

I. DEFINITIONS

The Hebrew word for "to sanctify" is *qadash,* which suggests the idea of "cutting" or separating. Separation, too, is the main idea of the New Testament word, *hagiazo.* The word *hagios* is related to *hagiazo,* and is usually translated "holy" or "sacred" and means quite literally to "set apart" something by or for God.

Thus a "sanctified" person is one who is separated from a sinful world and put into a special relationship to God. He is not *out* of the world, but while *in* it he is consecrated to God for divine service. A servant or slave

---

[1] Many terms or expressions are used for sanctification. Some are holiness, Christian perfection, perfect love, the deeper life, the baptism of the Holy Spirit, etc. All such terms are essentially synonymous, though there are varying shades of meaning and each term points up particular aspects or emphases of sanctification.

is *in* the world but separated from it to give his time and energies in the service of his master.

Now this "setting apart" represents the *outward* aspect of sanctification. The *inward* aspect has to do with the infilling of the Spirit of God, which means the increased activity of God within the person. It also means a fuller and richer extension of the love of God. It means, further, release to continuous growth in the things of the Spirit. And all of these characteristics of the Spirit-filled life have the aim of producing, in the person, power for witnessing and doing good works.

Also related to the *inward* aspect of sanctification is the cleansing from inward sin. If the infilling of the Spirit is the positive side of sanctification, the negative side is cleansing. Both occur in sanctification. The cleansed heart is nowhere more beautifully expressed than in Ezekiel 36:25–26: "I will sprinkle clean water upon you, and you shall be clean from all your uncleannesses, and from all your idols I will cleanse you. A new heart I will give you, and a new spirit I will put within you; and I will take out of your flesh the heart of stone and give you a heart of flesh." In verse 27 of the same chapter the positive side, or the infilling of the Spirit, is expressed: "And I will put my spirit within you, and cause you to walk in my statutes and be careful to observe my ordinances." (Compare Acts 2; Joel 2:28–32.)

Sanctification is wrought instantaneously, as John Wesley taught and as such modern thinkers as W. E. Sangster and Paul Rees teach. To everyone sanctification is a developing thing, but to some this growing aspect overshadows the instantaneous aspect. But there must be an initial infilling of the Spirit and cleansing from inward sin, which releases one to further advancement and growth in Christ Jesus.

The inner aspect, or what we have called the Spirit-filled life, is reflective of that quality known as holiness. Holiness is simply separation from the sinful world, with the divine enablement for holy or good living. This release of personality from the power of sin and to good living is reflected in Acts 26:18, where Paul says Jesus commissioned him to open men's eyes "that they may turn from darkness to light and from the power of Satan to God, that they may receive forgiveness of sins and a place among those who are sanctified by faith in me" (see also John 17:17; I Thessalonians 5:23).

With this groundwork laid, we are ready to come to our definition of sanctification. Perhaps it can best be defined in terms of its characteristics. A sanctified person is characterized by the fact that he is "set apart" or consecrated to the service of God; that he has been cleansed of sin; that he is the possessor of a new capacity for love and growth in love; that he has the power to witness and do good works; that he has victory over sin. And all these characteristics are produced by the Spirit Who dwells within.

II. A Word of Warning

A word of warning needs to be said here. The sanctified person has not "arrived." "Not that I . . . am already perfect," says St. Paul (Philippians 3:12). Once Spirit-filled, a person is only ready to grow to new heights in grace and knowledge of the truth. Rather than an *ending*, sanctification is a *beginning*. And what an exciting beginning it really is; for, once consecrated to do God's full will, one is ready to conquer new territory for

God. This conquering is filled with all the excitement and adventure of a mountaineer scaling a peak.

Do not suppose that sanctification will set you atop the peak all at once. Paul says, "I press on toward the goal for the prize of the upward call of God in Christ Jesus" (Philippians 3:14). Paul saw that sanctification was a growing, developing thing. Be patient; do not expect to arrive all at once. And above all, enter into the excitement of new discoveries as you scale the mountain of spiritual existence.

III. SENSING THE NEED FOR SANCTIFICATION

One cannot be filled with God's Spirit unless he wants to be, and he cannot want to be unless he sees his need.

A. Every Room Must Be Given Over to God

Conversion is an initial experience; we might say, the door leading into the Christian life. Conversion is repentance, issuing in forgiveness for past sins. Sanctification is more; it involves giving over to God every room of one's life. It is letting God's Spirit fill every room, nook, and cranny. Even some church-going people simply do not want to give up every room to God; they are selfish, wanting to keep the room of pleasure, power, or money for themselves. But the sanctified person gives over pleasure, power, money, and every other room of his life to the service of God. God demands every room.

Have you given over every room in your life to God? If you have not and are willing to admit that you have not, you see your need of sanctification.

B. Love and Witnessing

The chief characteristic of a Spirit-filled person is

love. His witnessing, his efforts for social reform are the product of love; they are not the product of duty or pride primarily, but of love.

When the Holy Spirit takes possession of every room of our lives, he casts out fear and puts in its place love (I John 4:18). This is a very big love indeed, for now one possesses an insatiable desire to learn all he can about God and to do all he can to bring others into the happiness God provides. This is why a man like John Wesley could say, "The world is my parish." Go to Westminster Abbey, London, and there you will see a memorial plaque to John Wesley. On the plaque he is depicted preaching to a crowd out-of-doors (his favorite place of preaching). He is unafraid; he is preaching out of a big heart of love. He is incurably desirous to see these men and women brought into a saving and satisfying knowledge of Jesus Christ. Riding into a certain town, John Wesley cried, "I came to bring them Christ." There you have it! The Spirit-filled person cannot keep still about Christ. Every nerve and fibre of his body is given over to the service of God; every ounce of his energy and strength is given in the work of God. Nothing pleases him more than to see a fellow brought into the Kingdom; nothing challenges him more than the fight for dying souls. He does not possess the Spirit; the Spirit possesses him and fills him with love and power to do a Kingdom-building task.

Now the question arises: "Do I have the Spirit in me in such degree? Does He so fill me that I have the courage, capacity, and the power to witness for Christ?" If the Spirit has possessed you and filled you with His love, the answer is "Yes." If He has not, do you see your need?

C. Power for Witnessing

Witnessing is telling the gospel story in word or deed or both. The question of power to witness is extremely important since the Christian Church is built on the principle of fellowship and the fellowship cannot grow unless Christians bring outsiders inside. To love and work to make outsiders insiders is the method of propagating the Christian Church.

This question of power to witness was so important that Jesus commanded the disciples to go everywhere preaching the gospel (Matthew 28:19–20). This was one of the last commands Jesus gave. But Jesus knew very well that the disciples could not preach or witness effectively in their own power. They simply did not have in themselves — even as we do not — the inner resources to witness and get results. Therefore, Jesus promised them — and us — help; that help was to be the Holy Spirit. In fact, before the Ascension Jesus told the disciples to wait in Jerusalem for the coming of the Holy Spirit. When He comes, said Jesus, "you shall receive power" to be "my witnesses . . . to the end of the earth" (Acts 1:8). The Greek word for power here is DUNAMIS, the word from which we get our English term, "dynamite." Thus, in our own language, we might well translate Acts 1:8 to read, "you shall receive the dynamite" of the Holy Spirit to witness. In more up-to-date language, "you shall receive the jet power" to blast off into a sinful stratosphere, to win men and women to Jesus Christ.

It was precisely this jet power which characterized that little band of apostles in the first century. Read the Acts of the Apostles and see for yourself! The activities and accomplishments of these Spirit-filled people are no less than astounding! Peter, John, Paul, Barnabas, and many others could not work hard enough, they could not do enough. The Spirit of God was in them, working in and through them, using them as instruments to win 3,000 converts (Acts 2:41), and "many day by day."

The fact that Christians can have power for witnessing has been summarized by James Stewart of Edinburgh in this beautifully descriptive statement: "It is a verifiable phenomenon of Christian experience that an individual man, laid hold upon by the Spirit of God, can have his whole life lifted to a level of spiritual force and efficiency which previously would have seemed quite incredible; and if the Spirit of God can do such mighty works for and in and by one life surrendered to His sway, what a revolutionizing of history might not result from a fully committed Church?"[2]

All this does not mean that you will necessarily win 3,000, 5,000, or any other number of people to Jesus Christ, though the influence of a Spirit-filled person continues and can never be measured. What it does mean is that the Spirit of God can lay hold on your life to work in and through you for whatever He desires to do and accomplish. Now the very personal question is just this: Have you been so laid hold upon by the Spirit of God? Have you received power for witnessing? If you have not, and if you are willing to admit that, you see your need of sanctification.

C. The Church's Greatest Need

There is no greater need in the Christian Church

---

[2] James S. Stewart, *Thine Is the Kingdom* (Edinburgh: The St. Andrew Press, 1956), p. 72.

today than a Spirit-filled people, possessing the power of God characteristic of first-century Christians. This is far more important than H bombs, rockets, or the establishing of a superior satellite system. It is more important than improving our education (and we need to do that in America!). The Spirit-filled life is more important than the solving of any problem current in our day or any day.

Why is Spirit-filled living so important? This is the only hope for making an unrighteous world better. Spirit-filled people are the life-blood of the Church. Spirit-filled people constitute the vehicle by which God builds His Church. Spirit-filled people can know and propagate victory over sin.

IV. A CO-OPERATIVE UNDERTAKING

Sanctified living is the product of both God's activity and man's effort. In other words, it is a co-operative undertaking.

A. God and Man at Work in Holy Living

St. Paul commands: "Bless them which persecute you" (Romans 12:14), and "Be of the same mind one toward another. . . . Be not wise in your own conceits. Recompense to no man evil for evil. Provide things honest in the sight of all men" (Romans 12:16–17). Micah 6:8 is a famous command to do good: "He hath showed thee, O man, what is good; and what doth the Lord require of thee, but to do justly, and to love mercy, and to walk humbly with thy God?"

The Bible is full of such injunctions. The command is clear: we must live holy lives. Now we have already said that holy lives cannot be lived if they are not Spirit-filled. Spirit-filling is God's part; but it is also plain from the Biblical commands that God presupposes effort on man's part too, otherwise there would be no sense in making commands. God does not do the whole job! It is possible to miss the mark of holy living by ignoring the promptings and refusing to tap the resources of the Spirit within us.

God's part in sanctification is made clear in I Thessalonians 5:23: "May the God of peace sanctify you wholly . . . ." Man's part is indicated in II Corinthians 7:1: " . . . let us cleanse ourselves from every defilement of body and spirit, and make holiness perfect in the fear of the Lord."

B.   John Wesley and Social Holiness

God commands in His Word that Christians produce good works. "By their fruits ye shall know them," said Jesus, and Romans 7:4 makes reference to bearing fruit for God. The natural product of faith and the Spirit-filled life is fruit. Without the Holy Spirit there can be little if any genuine fruit; with the Holy Spirit there inevitably comes much fruit.

John Wesley said, "There is no holiness without social holiness." This means that the test of sanctification is whether or not the Christian is actually contributing to a better world. Wesley took seriously the life of holiness: he helped the unemployed find jobs (he was known to have loaned money to get people started in business); he found housing for the homeless; he cared for the sick and dying; he encouraged prison reform; he advanced the notion of education for the masses; he cried out against the evils of alcoholic beverages; and we could go on! In fact, John Wesley took social holiness so seriously that J. Wesley Bready and others have pointed to him as the father of the social gospel movement of modern times.[3]

Wesley declared that it is not enough to think good thoughts and to hope for goodness. That is woefully inadequate! He said we must *be* good and *do* good. Such is certainly the command of Scripture: "As we have therefore opportunity, let us do good to all men, especially unto them who are of the household of faith" (Gal. 6:10). It is also confirmed in the lives of people truly Spirit-filled.

C. Practical Holiness

Now this business of being good and doing good points up the practical side of sanctification. There is no use testifying to the sanctified life if one is not doing all in one's power to improve the world around him. Indeed, if holiness is not a social thing, it is not holiness at all, and it is therefore blasphemy to testify to it.

Better still, avoid the risky business of boasting that you are holy, and simply let the fruit of a sanctified life show in active, continuous love for God and your neighbors. This is really what sanctification is all about anyway.

1. Scriptural Passages

To be read: Hebrews 12:12–17; Matthew 5:43–48; John 17:17–19; I Thessalonians 5:23–24; Philippians 3:12–16; I John 4:13–21; Acts 1:8; Acts 2; Romans 12:14–21.

---

[3] See John Wesley Bready, *This Freedom Whence?* (New York: American Tract Society, 1942). See also Timothy L. Smith, *Revivalism and Social Reform* (New York: Abingdon, 1958), a Ph.D. thesis at Harvard University which argues that social reform is a direct product of the movements of revivalism and perfectionism.

2. Bibliography

Berkhof, Louis. *Manual of Christian Doctrine*. Pp. 265-273.

Flew, R. Newton. *The Idea of Perfection in Christian Theology, An Historical Study of the Christian Ideal for the Present Life*. London: Oxford University Press, 1934.

Jones, E. Stanley. *Abundant Living*. Nashville: Abingdon, 1942. (A devotional guide.)

—————. *Victorious Living*. Nashville: Abingdon, 1936. (A valuable step-by-step guide into the experience of sanctification.)

Sangster, W. E. *The Path to Perfection*. Nashville: Abingdon, 1943.

—————. *The Pure in Heart, A Study in Christian Sanctity*. London: The Epworth Press, 1954.

Smith, Hannah Whitall. *The Christian's Secret of a Happy Life*. New York: Fleming H. Revell Co., 1941. (A book that has been of help to many people.)

Turner, George A. *The More Excellent Way*. Winona Lake: Light and Life Press, 1952.

Wiley, H. Orton. *Christian Theology*. Vol. III, chapter XXX.

3. Questions for Discussion

1. Define sanctification. Distinguish between the outward and inward aspects. Relate the infilling of the Spirit and cleansing.

2. What part does genuine love play in the sanctified life?

3. Do you really believe one can be laid hold on by the Spirit of God for witnessing?

4. Wherein can you co-operate with God in holy living? What is meant by social holiness?

12

The Sacrament of Baptism

In this chapter attention will be given to the sacrament of Baptism, and in the next to the sacrament of the Lord's Supper. But first we must make clear what a sacrament is and something of the Protestant view on the sacraments or ordinances.

A sacrament is, of course, something sacred, but its meaning goes far deeper than that. It is something special, and in Protestant theology the term is used in reference only to Baptism and the Lord's Supper. Both were instituted by Jesus Christ; both are outward signs[1] indicating an inward work wrought by divine grace; both inspire faith and obedience to God. It is a grave matter not to take their meaning seriously, and to neglect either is, as John Wesley said, to do so at one's own risk.

The Roman Catholics have seven sacraments: Baptism, the Lord's Supper, Confirmation, Penance, Extreme Unction, Ordination, and Matrimony. These seven, say the Catholics, are the specific God-ordained channels through which grace is given. Grace is not given out by indiscriminate means, they say, but through these seven means only.

113

Protestantism believes its two sacraments are means of grace, but not the exclusive means; and it rejects the other five which the Catholics hold. Protestantism traces its use of two sacraments to Old Testament days, when Circumcision and the Passover were the only sacramental act *per se*. "Circumcision," says Louis Berkhof, "was practiced among other nations as a measure of health, but among Israel it became a sacrament of the covenant of grace, symbolizing the cutting away of sin." Then Berkhof observes that in the days of Moses the "passover was added . . . , which symbolized and typified the deliverance of the people of God."[2] In the New Testament, Circumcision was replaced as a sacrament by Baptism, and the Passover by the Lord's Supper.

I. BAPTISM THE COMMAND OF JESUS CHRIST

After His resurrection, Christ instituted Baptism: "Go therefore and make disciples of all nations, baptizing them in the name of the Father and of the Son and of the Holy Spirit . . . " (Matthew 28:19). From the way this command to Baptism is carried out in the Acts of the Apostles, it is clear that the early Church considered it a means of witnessing to the fact that the person or household baptized had come into a new relationship with God.

Jesus Himself was baptized, and He saw the need for

---

[1] The Quakers and the Salvation Army claim to experience the Baptism of the Holy Spirit and the fellowship of communion without outward symbols and acts. Moreover, they do not allow the outward "sign." The Quakers, founded by George Fox, claim that the outward ritual and symbols of bread, wine, and water distract or get in the way of what the Spirit of God really wants to do for the person.

[2] Louis Berkhof, *Manual of Christian Doctrine*, p. 313.

the act as a witness, therefore He instituted it. That He did in fact institute Baptism is one reason it is considered a sacrament. The Lord's Supper was also instituted by Christ. Christians believe that part of the definition of a sacrament is that it was instituted by Christ Himself.

Now this command of Jesus to baptize was carried out in the early Church, as indicated in Acts 2. Peter announces, "Repent, and be baptized . . . for the forgiveness of your sins..." (verse 38). This emphasis on Baptism is typical of the first-century attitude. But the command to baptize was by no means limited to the first century; all through the history of the Church it has been followed and has been considered an important source of grace and a means of witnessing.

II. THE MEANING OF BAPTISM

What does Baptism really mean? What happens to the individual in Baptism? Questions such as these need an answer, and what is said in this section on the meaning of Baptism should help to clear up some of these queries.

A.   Baptism Is by Spirit and Water

Both Spirit and water are factors in Baptism. Upon believing, the Spirit of God regenerates (makes new or gives New Birth to) the person and ingrafts him into the true Church or Body of Christ (I Corinthians 12:13). Water Baptism helps identify him with Christ and shows the bond that exists between him and Christ. Baptism signifies the washing of regeneration (Titus 3:5), the forgiveness of sins (Acts 2:38), the New Birth (John 3:5). Baptism is, according to the Biblical view, essentially a spiritual act, and it is highly important to remember that it is essentially a spiritual act, something done to the heart or person himself.

But water plays a part too. It symbolizes, or makes clear by means of a material act, the fact of washing or cleansing from sin. So it is that we say that the water in Baptism symbolizes and seals the divine act already accomplished in the heart of the individual.

B. Baptism Is Done in the Name of the Trinity

Baptism is done in the name of the Father, Son, and Holy Spirit. This practice has been followed from very early times and stems from Jesus' command in Matthew 28:19.

C. The Place and Function of the Congregation in Baptism

Baptism is meaningful not only to the individual but to the congregation as well. In fact, the congregation is really promising to take the baptized person into its fellowship and to share in the responsibilities of his Christian nurture (Acts 2:42). Congregations should be reminded of their part in Baptism at every public service at which the sacrament is observed.

D. Baptism Is into Christ and His Church

Baptism is into Christ and therefore into His Church universal. One is not baptized a Presbyterian, Catholic, or Methodist; he is baptized a Christian. This is why re-baptism is a rare occurrence; at least it should be rare. It is even common for Catholics to recognize Protestant Baptism and vice versa. Moreover, if one has been baptized in a Methodist church, his Baptism holds good if he later joins the Presbyterian church. Baptism is into Christ, not into a denomination.

116

E. Death and Resurrection of the Person

Baptism signifies that one has died to sin and has been resurrected to new life in Christ Jesus. Romans 6 says, "Do you not know that all of us who have been baptized into Christ Jesus were baptized into his death? We were buried therefore with him by baptism into death, so that as Christ was raised from the dead by the glory of the Father, we too might walk in newness of life" (verses 3–4). In this Pauline figure of speech, we are reminded once again of the spiritual character of Baptism.

III. THE MODE OF BAPTISM CONSIDERED

Historically, three modes have been employed in Baptism: pouring, sprinkling, immersion. The Quakers have no outward mode; thus we could say that four general approaches, in terms of method, are used in the Christian Church.

A. The Relation of Meaning to Mode

The Quakers do the Christian world a great service by reminding us that the real meaning of Baptism is the important thing in Baptism. For the Quakers Baptism is an inner experience and is initiated by the Spirit Himself. The *meaning* of Baptism is thus emphasized over against the *rite* or *form*. It is generally accepted among Christians that meaning surpasses form in degree of importance. At the same time it is also generally accepted among Christians that we cannot dispense with outward modes and rituals.

B. Adult Baptism by Immersion

It is the conviction of the Baptist groups — and

others (e.g., the Disciples of Christ) — that the only proper mode of Baptism is by immersion. Romans 6 (the passage on death and resurrection through Baptism) makes sense and is really symbolized, say the immersionists, only when Baptism is done by immersion. It is further emphasized that the Greek word for baptize, BAPTIZO, means literally "to go down under," "to dip," "to submerge." (There are also other meanings of BAPTIZO.) Therefore, so the argument goes, this is the proper method.

A strong factor in support of this view is that immersion happens to be the only mode recognized as proper by all denominations; it is acceptable to all, while sprinkling and pouring are not.

Along with the immersion idea in Protestant circles goes the view that only adults may be baptized. In a word, the argument is that one cannot be baptized until he is old enough to "know" what he is doing; he must have the witness of the Spirit that he is a child of God before God can seal His promise of salvation to the individual in Baptism. This is called believer's Baptism.

Again it should be underscored that it is the real *meaning* of Baptism, rather than the mode, which is of supreme importance. Surely John Calvin caught the meaning of Baptism when he defined it as "a sign of initiation by which we are received into the fellowship of the Church, that, being grafted into Christ, we may be numbered among the children of God."[3]

C. Infant Baptism by Sprinkling

Infant Baptism is practiced by Methodists, Episcopalians, Presbyterians, and others. There are many arguments for infant Baptism. For one thing, whole households (including children very probably) were baptized according to the New Testament (see Acts 2:39; 16:15, 33; 18:8; I Corinthians 1:16). This appears to be a perfectly normal thing and was done repeatedly in the first-century Church. D. M. Baillie says that "to a Jew it would seem the most natural thing in the world that when a man became a Christian he should have his children baptized as well as himself, just as he had his sons circumcised in their infancy . . . . "[4]

A further argument for infant Baptism is that we have historic evidence that children were baptized in the second century,[5] thus giving ancient backing to the tradition. Still another argument is that Jesus said, "Let the children come to me, and do not hinder them; for to such belongs the kingdom of heaven" (Matthew 19:14), thus suggesting that it would not be in the spirit of Christ to refuse infants Baptism.[6] Another argument for the Baptism of infants, is given strong emphasis by theologians of the Reformed and covenant tradition, namely that, "We are not taught, either by word or example, that persons born and reared in Christian families may not be baptized until they have come to years . . . and have professed their faith in Christ."[7]

The most thorough study and research in favor of infant Baptism which has come out in recent years is that done by the Swiss theologian, Oscar Cullmann. His

---

[3] John Calvin, *Institutes*, IV, xv, 1.

[4] Donald M. Baillie, *The Theology of the Sacraments* (New York: Scribner's, 1957), p. 83.

[5] Berkhof, *op. cit.*, p. 321.

[6] It is interesting that this verse sometimes appears on the baptismal font in churches practicing infant Baptism.

[7] Berkhof, *loc. cit.*

findings are recorded in the invaluable little book, *Baptism in the New Testament,* which should be read by those wishing to do further reading on infant Baptism.[8]

It is the belief of those who practice infant Baptism that something is accomplished in three directions: (1) the child himself is blessed, (2) the parents make a promise, (3) the congregation makes a promise. As to the *child,* it is believed by many that in some mystical way God strengthens faith in that child of Christian parents. It is never assumed by those who practice infant Baptism that the means of grace are limited to the moment of Baptism; rather, it is felt that, when the child grows older and is told what has happened to him, he will be inspired to decide for Christ and be spurred on in the faith.

As to the *parents,* it is made clear to them that they will teach both the Old and New Testament Scriptures to the child and that they will do everything in their power to bring up that child in the "admonition and nurture of the Lord." In other words, Baptism is something which puts a good deal of responsibility on the parents.

This business of responsibility, however, is not limited to the parents; it is laid upon the *congregation* as well. When the members of the congregation witness infant Baptism, they are promising and announcing that they, too, will do all they can to rear this child in the "admonition and nurture" of the Lord. Church members should be eager and willing to teach a Sunday school class, work in the junior church, or do whatever they can

---

[8] Oscar Cullmann, *Baptism in the New Testament* (Chicago: Henry Regnery Company, 1950), p. 70 for a summary of his conclusions.

for the upbuilding of the precious little children of their congregation.

A word should be added here with reference to adults who are baptized in churches which practice infant Baptism. In many of these churches Baptism can be by either sprinkling or immersion, at the discretion of the person being baptized. The candidate for baptism ought, by all means, to counsel with his pastor before being baptized.

Summary

It is interesting that the immersionists are "dedicating" their infants in many churches. This points up the fact that they feel the need of calling parents and congregation to their tasks of rearing the children in the things of God. It is also believed that God would not withhold His blessing from a child until immersion.

Further, and on the other side of the question is the fact that it is increasingly held that infant Baptism is not sufficient in itself. It must be followed by nurture, education, and confirmation or the like. Thus it is absolutely necessary that a person baptized in infancy realize that he must make his decision for Christ at a responsible age.

1. Scriptural Passages

To be read: Acts 1:4–5, 8; 2:37–42; 16:31–34; 18:8; I Corinthians 12:12–13; Titus 3:1–7; John 3:1–21; Matthew 28:16–20; Romans 6:1–11; Galatians 3:23–29; I Peter 3:18–22; Colossians 2:11–15.

2. Bibliography

Baillie, D. M. *The Theology of the Sacraments.* New York: Charles Scribner's Sons, 1957. Lecture III.

Berkhof, Louis. *Manual of Christian Doctrine.* Pp. 315–323.

Cullmann, Oscar. *Baptism in the New Testament.* Translated by

J. K. S. Reid. Chicago: Henry Regnery Company, 1950.

Kennedy, H. A. A. *The Theology of the Epistles*. London: Duckworth, 1919 (1948). Pp. 150–151.

Lampe, G. W. H. *The Seal of the Spirit*. New York: Longmans, 1951. (For the advanced student.)

Whale, J. S. *Christian Doctrine*. Pp. 155–166.

Wiley, H. Orton. *Christian Theology*. Vol. III, pp. 155–189.

3. Questions for Discussion

1. What do we mean by the term "sacrament"?
2. How many and what are the sacraments according to Protestant theology? According to Roman Catholic theology?
3. Discuss the meanings of Baptism.
4. What is the relation of *meaning* and *mode* in Baptism?
5. Discuss the position of adult or believer's Baptism by immersion. Discuss the position of infant Baptism by sprinkling. What Biblical evidence is there for each position?

13

The Sacrament of
The Lord's Supper

Like Baptism, the Lord's Supper is a sacrament. It was instituted by Jesus (Matthew 26:26–29; Mark 14:22–25; Luke 22:19–20; I Corinthians 11:23–25); it is an avenue of divine grace when properly observed; it is executed by outward and visible signs (the bread and wine); it signifies an inner work in the individual who partakes.

The Lord's Supper was celebrated probably at a meal (called the AGAPE) in ancient times (Matthew 26; I Corinthians 11), and is the New Testament replacement of the Passover meal in the Old Testament.[1] Some Christians still celebrate the Lord's Supper with a simple meal (Church of the Brethren, which combines feet-washing with the meal), but usually the morsel of bread and the bit of wine[2] are now used in place of the meal.

---

[1] On the question, "Was the Last Supper a Passover Meal?" see Joachim Jeremias, *The Eucharistic Words of Jesus* (New York: The Macmillan Company, 1955), chapter 1.

[2] Referring to the drink at the Supper, our Lord used the expression, "the fruit of the vine." For a discussion of the wine itself, see Jeremias, *Ibid.*, pp. 27–29.

I. WHAT THE LORD'S SUPPER SIGNIFIES

The Lord's Supper signifies several very specific things. These must be made clear and must be kept clearly in mind.

A. The Cross and Sufferings of Christ Are Signified

The broken bread serves to remind the partaker of the broken body of Jesus on the cross, while the wine is a reminder of His shed blood. The Supper should be a sharp reminder of the extreme suffering of Christ,[3] thus evoking love in the heart and increased appreciation for the benefits of the Atonement. Indeed, the Lord's Supper signifies that the redemptive work was actually accomplished. When one partakes of the bread and wine he is partaking symbolically of the crucified Christ; that is to say, the individual personally benefits from the cross, the love given and demonstrated, and the salvation offered.

B. Spiritual Vitality Is Signified

When one takes the elements of bread and wine in faith, he is symbolizing the fact that God feeds the soul. Even as bread and drink rejuvenate and strengthen the physical body, so in the bread and wine God gives life, strength, and joy to the spiritual part of the person.

C. The Communion of Believers Is Signified

Sometimes we call the Lord's Supper the "Communion." Why? Because it symbolizes, emphasizes, and reminds us of the fact that we live in a community, a

---

[3] For a description of the sufferings of Christ, see the chapter on the cross.

community of believers called the Church. The sacrament symbolizes the "togetherness" of Christians; it demonstrates our oneness in Christ and increases our sense of fellowship. " . . . We who are many are one body, for we all partake of the same loaf" (I Corinthians 10:17).

One must never partake at the table of the Lord with malice toward a brother (see Matthew 5:23–24). True Christians are one in Christ under His cross, for all participate equally in the benefits of the Christ and His cross. Race, color, or denomination are not discriminating factors. True Christians are one in Him and the celebration of the Supper reminds us of this significant fact. Further, it is a sharp prod to the participator to do his part in maintaining oneness and harmony in the Church.

D. The Lord's Supper Is a Sign of His Coming

Christ Himself associated His second coming and His triumph with the Supper (Mark 14:25; Matthew 26:29; Luke 22:15–18), and St. Paul says, "For as often as you eat this bread and drink the cup, you proclaim the Lord's death *until he comes*" (I Corinthians 11:26). The Lord's Supper is to be considered an important activity in the interval between His death and return. It is a reminder not only of His death but also that He will in fact come again.

II. THE PRESENCE OF CHRIST IN HIS SUPPER

Is Christ present in His Supper? Christians agree that Christ or His Spirit is somehow present. Historically this doctrine of the presence of Christ in the Supper is called the "Real Presence." But *how* is He really present in the Supper? Four major answers have been given to this question.

A. Calvin: The Mystical Presence

The first answer to consider is that given by John Calvin. He said that Christ was in the Supper in a spiritual sense. In some mystical but real way, Christ is in and communing with the partaker. Calvin said further that the Supper was a pledge to the believer that God did a work for him. The values of the cross and its results are present in the sacrament and are actually applied to the believing heart.

B. Zwingli: A Memorial

Zwingli, like Calvin, was a Swiss reformer of the sixteenth century. But he was unlike Calvin in his view of the presence of Christ in the sacramental Supper. To Zwingli, the emphasis was not to be put on the presence of Christ so much as on the Supper as a memorial of Christ's death and sufferings. To take the bread and wine was to witness to the fact that the participator had surrendered to the Christ of the cross. Zwingli placed little emphasis on what the sacrament itself does for the believer, but much emphasis on the idea of a memorial of Christ's death.

C. The Roman Catholic Church: Transubstantiation

The Roman Catholic view of Christ's presence is called transubstantiation. By this is meant that Christ is actually and physically in the bread and wine. The words of Jesus, "This is my body" (Matthew 26:26), are taken quite literally, and Catholics believe the bread in the Eucharist (Lord's Supper) actually turns to Christ's body and that the wine really becomes His blood. Support for this view is found in the Catholic interpretation of John chapter 6 where Jesus says, "I am the bread of life," and "I am the living bread. . . . " (verses 48 and 51), which words are, like Matthew 26:26, taken literally.

Now to hold to this position, Catholics have to juggle their ideas a good bit. They juggle them in this manner: When the priest blesses the elements, it is said, to all *outward appearances* the bread and wine remain the same. The characteristics of smell, touch, and taste remain unaltered. But the *substance* of the elements changes into actual flesh and blood, the flesh and blood of Christ. Obviously, they distinguish between *substance* and *outward appearance* or what are called attributes (physical characteristics).

To a host of people, Catholics have been unsuccessful in explaining how the bread and wine can change without *appearing* to do so.

D. Luther: Consubstantiation

Martin Luther's view, occasionally modified by Lutherans today, is called not transubstantiation but consubstantiation. Luther held that, while the bread and wine remain bread and wine, Christ, His blood and body, are actually *with* (*con* means "with") and *in* the bread and wine. Thus the partaker really receives the body and blood of our Lord which nourishes his spirit. It is believed that Christ accompanies the bread and wine in a quite literal and local sense; He is really there.

E. Conclusion

Many Presbyterians and others would say Calvin has come the closest to the Scriptural view of the Real Presence of Christ in the Supper. Most Baptists believe

Zwingli's "memorial" position is more nearly correct. Roman and Eastern Catholics accept the view of transubstantiation. Most Lutherans accept the consubstantiational view. But whatever the view, all agree that in some way Christ is present in His supper.

That God in Christ is really present in the Supper is perhaps more easily understood if we remind ourselves of the doctrine of the omnipresence of God. We say that God is everywhere, not so much *in* as transcending space and things. Further, Jesus said, "Where two or three are gathered in my name, there am I in the midst of them" (Matthew 18:20). Now God is everywhere, and He is present "where two or three are gathered" for worship, and in the Lord's Supper He is present in a very special way. Donald Baillie, in the helpful book, *The Theology of the Sacraments,* says of the Lord's Supper: "the God Who was incarnate in Jesus uses the symbolism of the sacrament as a special means of awakening the faith of His people that they may receive Him, since faith is the channel by which God's most intimate presence comes to men in this earthly life."[4] To Professor Baillie's fine statement we can add this, that the Holy Spirit applies and makes real to the partaker's heart the Real Presence of Christ.

III. TAKING THE LORD'S SUPPER SERIOUSLY

It is a grave error to take lightly the Lord's Supper, for it is a highly sacred affair and can be most meaningful if one is properly prepared to take it.

---

[4] Donald Baillie, *The Theology of the Sacraments* (New York: Scribner's, 1957), p. 99.

A. The Word and the Sacrament

Both the sacrament and the Word are vehicles of the same divine grace. The sacrament only extends and adds to the effectiveness of God's Word in the life of the believer. Both the Word and the sacrament bring one closer to Christ. Both feed the soul, both add spiritual vitality, both increase the sense of the Spirit within.

Now if we should take God's Word seriously, we should also take the Lord's Supper seriously. Yet how often do we take the Supper as a mere matter of course, our minds flitting from one thing to another. It is no wonder we hear the complaint that the Supper is unmeaningful! If one does not listen to the Word, he cannot benefit by it; by the same token, if one does not come to the Table of the Lord in an attitude of meditation and expectation, he cannot profit by this source of offered grace.

B. Self-examination and the Lord's Supper

What can the partaker do to make the Lord's Supper more meaningful? When one comes to the table, he must be prepared in the following ways. (1) First and foremost, he must be a believer in Christ Jesus. Paul says, "Any one who eats and drinks without discerning the body eats and drinks judgment upon himself" (I Corinthians 11:29). The *Didache,* a Christian document dating around A.D. 100, states: "If any man is holy, let him come [to the Table of the Lord]; if any is not, let him repent." (2) Secondly, if perchance someone is out of harmony with a brother in the Church, he must ask forgiveness, reconciling himself to his fellow, before he can come to the Table (see Matthew 5:23–24). One of the purposes of serving Holy Communion is to maintain harmony in the Church. (3) Finally, a highly important function of preparation has to do with attitude. One must come to the table of our Lord in a spirit of real meditation and reverence, *expecting* — that is an important word — that God will reveal Himself *to us* in His own way and meet our individual needs.

1. Scriptural Passages

To be read: Matthew 26:26–29; Mark 14:22–25; Luke 22:19–20; I Corinthians 10:16–17; 11:23–25; Matthew 18:15–20; 5:21–26.

2. Bibliography

Baillie, D. M. *The Theology of the Sacraments and Other Papers,* with a biographical essay by John Baillie. New York: Charles Scribner's Sons, 1957.

Berkhof, Louis, *Manual of Christian Doctrine*. Grand Rapids: Wm. B. Eerdmans Publishing Company, 1953.

Jeremias, Joachim. *The Eucharistic Words of Jesus,* translated from the second German edition by Arnold Ehrhardt. New York: The Macmillan Company, 1955. (For the advanced student.)

Kennedy, H. A. A. *The Theology of the Epistles*. London: Duckworth, 1919 (1948). Pp. 151–152.

Whale, J. S. *Christian Doctrine*. Pp. 166–169.

Wiley, H. Orton. *Christian Theology*. Vol. III, pp. 189–208.

3. Questions for Discussion

1. The Lord's Supper signifies what things?
2. Summarize the four positions on the Real Presence. Toward which do you lean? Why?
3. In what ways must one prepare himself for taking the Lord's Supper?

14

Immortality and The Things To Come

What happens to us after death? To this question we direct our attention now.

I. THE REALITY OF DEATH

Physical death is a reality. Some of the religious cults try to make us deny the fact of death. But if death is not real, where are our friends and loved ones who were once with us? They simply are not here any longer; they are in fact dead physically.

A. Death and Punishment

The Scriptures teach that death is not only a fact — the real separation of body and soul — but also that it is punishment for sin. " . . . As sin came into the world through one man and death through sin, and so death spread to all men because all men sinned . . . ," says Paul in Romans 5:12 (cf. Romans 5:17). And in Romans 6:23 Paul says that "the wages of sin is death . . . " (see also I Corinthians 15:21–22).

B. The Wholesome Influence of Death

In spite of the fact that death is a real and terrible

fact, it has its benefits in the community. Death is a sober reminder to everyone, sinner and believer alike. It reminds us all that this life on earth is temporary; it reminds us that we need always to be ready to die; and it reminds us that money, power, or prestige are not eternal and therefore not the most important things of life. Death brings men face to face with eternal values and verities. This is why attending a funeral tends to sift out of our thinking superfluous ideas and ambitions and helps re-orientate us to noble life goals.[1]

II. THE SPIRIT NEVER DIES

The spirit — that something that gives and is life, that causes movement and speech — never dies. The body dies, but not the inner person or spirit. Physical death does not end the life principle of the person himself. Physical death is only one step in the ongoing and eternal process of conscious life. It would be well for you to read in this connection I Corinthians 15.

A. Some False Notions about What Happens to the Spirit after Death

1. PURGATORY

A false doctrine taught by Catholics is that of purgatory. It is believed that upon death one goes to purgatory unless he is good enough to enter immediately into heaven. Most are not so good, say Catholics, and

---

[1] It is hoped by many that funerals will never cease to be public affairs, and it is further desired that the church funerals will continue. The Church is a community center, and the great religious events of life—Baptism or dedication at infancy, confirmation and/or Church membership, marriage, death, etc.—need to be materially identified with the Church for emphasis and public witness.

therefore must work out their salvation in purgatory through suffering and a process of purification. The prayers and good works of Christians living on earth can shorten the time a friend or loved one stays in purgatory.

There is, however, no real Scriptural support for this doctrine (though some passages are cited as supporting this belief — e.g., Isaiah 4:4; Matthew 12:32). The chief support is found in II Maccabees 12:43, 45, where mention is made of making sacrifices and prayers for the dead, "that they may be loosed from sins." From this, Catholics have jumped to the conclusion that there must be a purgatory out of which people can be prayed and released. But II Maccabees is a non-canonical book; that is, it is not accepted as part of the authentic Scriptures by Protestants.

2. THE CATHOLIC VIEW OF THE DEATH OF UNBAPTIZED BABIES

Babies who die unbaptized, say Catholics, go to a place called *limbus infantum*. These infants can never get into heaven because they have not fulfilled the Biblical command to be baptized with water and the Spirit (John 3:5). They are thus deprived of heaven, but it is suggested that they do not suffer pain or torture.

3. THE CATHOLIC VIEW ON OLD TESTAMENT BELIEVERS

Those who died before Christ and who were good Hebrew believers went to a place called *limbus patrum*. Catholics say that Christ, after His death, went to this place and took these believers to heaven.

4. SOUL SLEEP

Some sects believe that upon death one's soul "sleeps" until the General Resurrection and Judgment. The soul is alive, to be sure, but unconscious. Some accept this doctrine on the basis that, when the Bible speaks of death, it often refers to death as "sleep" (see, for example, the account of Stephen's death, Acts 7:60). But the orthodox position is that sleep is a figure for death. It is further made clear in the Bible that believers, upon death, go immediately and consciously into the presence of their Lord. The story of the rich man and Lazarus (Luke 16:19ff.) documents this truth (see also Philippians 1:23).

5. ANNIHILATION

Then there are those who believe that the wicked are annihilated, that is, destroyed. The passages using such terms as "death" or "destruction" are taken to mean that a person's soul ceases to exist at death and that cessation of soul is, in itself, punishment ("hell") for unbelief.

But the Bible makes clear the fact that sinners exist forever (Matthew 25:46).

6. SECOND CHANCE

This doctrine teaches that after death every unbeliever will be given one more and final chance to decide for or against Christ. This will happen before the General Resurrection and Judgment. Some believe that those who have died in their sins will go to hell itself, but that hell is no more than a school to prepare one for heaven. Others are vague about the state of an unbeliever at death, and state only that God will give them a second chance to get into heaven. But the Scriptures are clear in teaching that the state of a believer is settled at death (Luke 16:19–31).

7. THE DENIAL OF HELL

There are those who deny hell altogether. The denial is based on the belief that hell is merely an idea which grew up in the mind of the race (the same explanation is given of the devil, who also is a mere "idea"). "But hell itself does not exist," they say. It is argued that a kind and good God would not allow anyone to suffer eternal punishment. In fact, all will go to heaven. This is called the doctrine of universalism. But the plain teaching of Scripture is that there is a heaven and that there is a hell, and that, while some will go to heaven, others will in fact go to hell (cf. Matthew 10:28; Luke 12:5; Matthew 5:3, 12, 20; Mark 10:21).

8. Denial of Both Heaven and Hell

Certain thinkers deny any life after death. "Death ends all," they say. At best, immortality is social; that is, one's name, memory and influence are carried on in the human race. It is claimed that there is no demonstrable evidence for life after death. That is, we cannot actually show "proof positive" that the person or spirit lives on. Of course, one who does not believe the Scriptures could come to such a conclusion though there are some most convincing philosophic arguments for immortality. Time and space do not permit outlining all the philosophic and psychological arguments for immortality, but perhaps C. S. Lewis has brought into focus one of the best arguments of all: "The Christian says, 'Creatures are not born with desires unless satisfaction for those desires exists.' A baby feels hunger: well, there is such a thing as food. A duckling wants to swim: well, there is such a thing as water . . . If I find in myself a desire which no experience in this world can satisfy, the most probable explanation is that I was made for another world."[2]

---

[2] C. S. Lewis, *Mere Christianity*, p. 118.

B.   Conclusion and Summary

All the answers about what happens to us after death are not given us in the Bible. It is really not necessary that we be told any more. But the Scripture does teach that there is a heaven and a hell and that the spirit will enter the one or the other, depending on one's relationship with God at death. The Bible also teaches that where one goes at death he will remain for eternity.

III. THE SECOND COMING, GENERAL RESURRECTION AND FINAL JUDGMENT

There is another dimension to immortality which is also clearly taught in Scripture. That has to do with the Second Coming of our Lord, at which time the General Resurrection of the dead and their final Judgment will take place.

A.   The Second Coming Based on Scripture

The Bible clearly teaches that Christ will come again. In fact, there is a strong emphasis on the Second Coming in the New Testament. Jesus referred to His own Second Coming (Matthew 24:30; 25:31; 26:64). Acts 1:11 is a famous promise of His Second Coming, and the fact is referred to in the Epistles (I Thessalonians 4:15, 16; Hebrews 9:28; etc.). The Scripture teaches that He will come suddenly, perhaps when we least expect Him (Matthew 24:40–42, 44, I Thessalonians 5:2), and that He will return in person (Acts 1:11).

What should be our twentieth century attitude toward this scriptural doctrine? It should not be one of "date-setting"; no one knows the hour of His coming (Mark 13:32; Luke 12:40), and it is not the Christian's business to concern himself with the time. His task is to be prepared (Mark 13:33; Luke 12:35–40) and to invite others to ready themselves. Furthermore, the Christian's attitude should not only be one of readiness rather than "date-setting," but one of hope rather than gloom. Christians in modern times have often been fearful in looking toward the Second Coming. But the New Testament teaching was given for the *encouragement* of first-century Christians. Someone has suggested that early Christians said first thing in the morning, "This may be the day!" What a thrill if Christ would come today! they thought. We too should have this attitude, for when He comes our earthly trials and sufferings will terminate, and only then will life be lived at its fullest.

B. The Resurrection and Judgment

Now the purpose of Jesus' Second Coming is to set up the future and eternal Kingdom of God, of which all believers will be a part. At His appearing He will resurrect the dead (Matthew 22:23ff.) and pass final judgment on everyone (John 5:28–29). The resurrection will be bodily, and the body will be real but spiritual (I Corinthians 15), apparently the same kind of a body Christ had after His resurrection (Philippians 3:21).

Christ will be the Judge of the resurrected (Matthew 25:31–32), and He will judge everyone who has ever lived (Matthew 25:32). Christ will be a fair Judge, judging according to the degree of light each has had. And apparently there will be rewards for the righteous and degrees of punishment for the unrighteous (Matthew 11:24; Luke 12:47–48; 20:47).

C. Heaven and Hell

After the Judgment, Christ will give each person

his due reward in heaven or hell as the case may be (Matthew 25:46). Now heaven and hell are real places, and they are quite opposite. In the one there is fellowship with God, in the other total absence from God, which is the essence of hell, even as the essence of heaven is communion with God. In the one there is perfection, in the other utter frustration. The one is of the nature of construction, integration, and all that is good; the other is of the nature of destruction, maladjustment, and all that is bad.

This is the important thing to remember: the key to heaven is in accepting Christ as personal Lord and Savior and in producing the fruit of the life in Christ.

1. Scriptural Passages

To be read: Romans 5:12–21; 6:23; I Corinthians 15:21–22; Luke 16:19–31; Mark 13; Luke 12:35–48; John 5:25–29; Philippians 3:17–21; Matthew 25:31–46; 11:22–24; Hebrews 9:28; Acts 1:9–11; I Timothy 6:14; I Thessalonians 1:5–2:15.

2. Bibliography

Berkhof, Louis. *Manual of Christian Doctrine.* Pp. 333–361.

Jones, Russell Bradley. *A Survey of the Old and New Testaments.* Grand Rapids: Baker Book House, 1957. Chapter 17.

Whale, J. S. *Christian Doctrine.* Chapter VIII.

Wiley, H. Orton. *Christian Theology.* Vol. III, Part VI, "The Doctrine of Last Things."

3. Questions for Discussion

1. Can you suggest some wholesome reminders that come to us in the presence of death?
2. Review the false teachings about what happens to us after death.
3. What will happen at the Second Coming?
4. Review C. S. Lewis' argument for life after death.

Index